86400

86400

Manage Your Purpose to Make Every Second of Each Day Count

LAVAILLE
LAVETTE

NEW YORK   BOSTON   NASHVILLE

Unless otherwise noted, Scripture quoted from the Holy Bible, New International Version R, copyright © 1973, 1978, 1984 by International Bible Society. Used by permission of Zondervan Publishing House. All rights reserved.

Scripture quotations marked (KJV) are taken from the King James Version of the Holy Bible, copyright © 1973, Broadman Press. All rights reserved. Published by Holman Bible Publishers, Nashville, TN 37234. Printed in the USA, ISBN 1-55819-250-6.

New Advent: The Holy Bible, Old Testament first published 1609 by the English College at Douay. New Testament first published 1582 by the English College at Rheims. Revised and annotated 1749 by Bishop Richard Challoner. Online edition copyright © 2006 by Kevin Knight, Imprimatur. +James Cardinal Gibbons, Archbishop of Baltimore, September 1, 1899.

FaithWords
Hachette Book Group
237 Park Avenue
New York, NY 10017

www.faithwords.com

Printed in the United States of America

First Edition: March 2011
10 9 8 7 6 5 4 3 2 1

FaithWords is a division of Hachette Book Group, Inc.
The FaithWords name and logo are trademarks of Hachette Book Group, Inc.

The publisher is not responsible for websites (or their content) that are not owned by the publisher.

Library of Congress Cataloging-in-Publication Data

Lavette, Lavaille.
   86400 : manage your purpose to make every second of each day count / Lavaille Lavette. — 1st ed.
      p. cm.
   ISBN 978-0-446-57147-0
   1. Time management—Religious aspects—Christianity. I. Title.
   II. Title: Manage your purpose to make every second of each day count.
   BV4598.5.L38 2011
   248.4—dc22

                                                          2010048151

This book is dedicated to my loving mother and father, Hazel and Jimmie Red, and to those who were part of the village that helped to raise me, especially my grandmother Josephine "Mini" Red and my aunt Helen Williams.

Acknowledgments

Thank you, God, for entrusting me with your daily gift of 86400 Seconds.

Thank you to my childhood pastor Rev. Wilton Thomas and to pastors Kirbyjon Caldwell, Joel Osteen, Dr. Ed and Lady Saundra Montgomery, T. D. Jakes, Charles Stanley, Paula White, Rudy Rasmus, Marcos Witt, Ed Young, Dr. Ronnie Floyd, Bishop Charles Blake, Sr., and Rick Warren for whom I draw spiritual insight and inspiration.

A special thank-you to my grade school teachers; Ms. Yvonne Thierry Johnson, Ms. Mary Ellen Donatto, Sister Aquinas, S.S.F., Sister Letitia Senegal, S.S.F., Sister Marie Antonia Rideaux, S.S.F., Dr. Rodney Johnson, Mr. Charles Ruffino, and Ms. Rebecca Sylvester.

A huge thank-you to all of the wonderful 86400 Advisers for sharing your insight, time and wisdom; Rudy Ramus, Marcos Witt, Paula White, Greg Baldwin, Ralph de la Vega, Coach Les Miles, Sherri Shepherd, Don Fertman, Dennis Devorick, Twiler Portis, Elvin Hayes, David Brokaw, Ricky Anderson, Federico Compean, Daymond Johns, Roland Martin, Jamie Foster Brown, Alana Stewart, Bill Cosby, and Mike Feinberg.

A special thank-you to David Dunham, Harry Helm, Rolf Zettersten, Adrienne Ingrum, Ada Edwards, Cynthia

Cooper, Dr. Louella Riggs-Cook, AnnMarie Wallace, Howard Middleton, Dr. Rod Paige, and all the 86400 Movement supporters for believing in this project. Thank you Aswad Walker for your dedication and input. Thank you to Angela P. Dodson, Megan Byrd, and Adlai Yeomans for your assistance.

Last but certainly not least, I want to thank all of my family members for blessing me with their encouragement, prayers, and support. I especially want to thank; my husband, John Thibodeaux, my mother, Hazel Red, my aunt Helen Williams, for your input and the hours you all spent reading and re-reading this manuscript. To my niece Katie Red thanks for all your questions, and to my cousins Antonio Velasquez, Jacy Davis, my aunts Lillian Davis, Jeanette Bougere, Alice Antione, Betty Cornish, my brothers Gregory Red, Tyrone Red, my father-in-law, Manuel Thibodeaux, mother-in-law Louvanna Thibodeaux, sister-in-law Tina Red and my uncles Gerald Williams, Plummer Stephens, Clayton Davis, thank you for all of your support.

Remember that together, we can make a difference and be the difference in our lives and the lives of so many others.

Contents

THE LIFE WE'RE INTENDED TO LEAD   171

Introduction: From Time Management to Purpose Management

Our quest as humans, as followers of Christ, is to discern the value of a day, of a moment, and fill it with unique purpose. Each day has 86400 seconds—60 seconds in a minute, 60 minutes in an hour, and 24 hours in a day, a total of 1440 minutes or 86400 seconds—in it. Each of those seconds is a promise of God's glory for our lives.

Leaders of a national denomination had gathered to focus on making their church more effective at meeting the everyday needs of members and their communities. As it was related to me by a minister friend, the presiding bishop asked a simple question: "Just what is it that we're doing on a daily basis?" The ministers responded with a laundry list of tasks and assignments. The activities they included showed that they were busy, but few of their activities had much to do with service to their congregations or others.

"It seems we're so busy we can't get anything done," the bishop responded.

What he said in brief, brilliant elegance was that his team of ministers had done well at managing their time, but failed at managing their purpose.

Managing your purpose involves exercising control of your actions to carry out a plan to achieve an anticipated outcome or desired effect. Purpose management is a continuing cycle that engages you in activities that are relevant to the fulfillment of your purpose.

"Don't say you don't have enough time," H. Jackson Brown, Jr., the *New York Times* best-selling author wrote in *Life's Little Instruction Book* (Thomas Nelson, 2000). "You have exactly the same number of hours per day that were given to Helen Keller, Louis Pasteur, Michelangelo, Mother Teresa, Leonardo da Vinci, Thomas Jefferson, and Albert Einstein." To that list, Brown could have added the modern-day likes of Oprah, President Barack Obama, Brad Pitt, Peyton Manning, Bill Gates, and Steve Harvey.

What did Keller, Pasteur, and Einstein do with their 86400 seconds that we can learn to do? They maximized the time they engaged in activities that reflected their passions and their purpose. They lived lives of purpose. Our seconds are as valuable as theirs, and we have the same ability to make the difference and be the difference.

What is needed for us to get the most out of our lives as did Michelangelo, Da Vinci, and Einstein is a focus on purpose management.

This book is not a new lesson or concept on time management. We all have just 86400 seconds each day. This book is not a manual to help you divide your day into seconds in order to be a better multitasker. It's not a fresh new approach to time management for the digital age. I'm not knocking time-management information; some of it has a useful place in your life. When I came across the notion of my day being broken down into its smallest form, seconds—86400 seconds, to be exact—I experienced an awakening. The 86400 concept, quite simply, struck a resounding chord in me. This book is an instigator for making the most of your God-given time.

Managing your time effectively will aid you in getting things done. However, focusing strictly on time management will allow you to be more efficient only at what you are already doing. Purpose management challenges you to use those precious 86400 seconds you are given each day in a way that allows you to live your passion, achieve your goals, and become all that the Creator ordained you to be.

We all have the responsibility and privilege to take advantage of the time we are given. No more "I'll do that tomorrow." No more "It's too late." Every single person, no matter how old or young, how poor or rich, has the opportunity to forgo complacency and claim a life of intention and vision. A life of such deliberate renewal may seem unattainable if you don't know where to start.

When I was trying, like so many others, to get a handle on how I spent my days, I got as many time-management books as I could find—from planners to journals. I even bought timers. I accumulated so much information on the topic that I began to conduct time-management workshops. Some of the time-management methods helped me to pack more into my day. Other techniques helped me to keep track of all that I had packed into my day. These tools even gave me a temporary sense of accomplishment, especially when I could mark off my list the things I was able to finish, but, as time progressed, I would go back to my old habits of spending too little time on things that were important and too much time on things that weren't.

I treated time management as I would a fad diet. I've had enough experience with weight-loss regimens of all sorts to know that treating time management as if it were the grapefruit diet or the cabbage soup diet would not help me achieve my ideal life. Neither diet helped me maintain an ideal weight, and time-management fads would not maximize my time and fulfill my purpose. Only when I was able to make a change in my eating habits that was natural and sustainable was I able to achieve my weight goal.

The same approach helped me maximize my daily 86400 seconds. I found it hard to be fulfilled crossing tasks off a checklist or going about my day as if I was the character Jack Bauer from the TV show *24*, always racing against time, beholden to what I had to get done before the clock ticked down to zero. Managing career, family, and community responsibilities was overwhelming for me. Just as I had a breakthrough with my diet, I had a breakthrough several years ago with how I spent my 86400s, my days. I was able to weave together a life that was overflowing with intention and relevance. It was natural and sustainable. My life ultimately made sense as I began to make the most of my 86400s, my God-given time. The time, the days, the seconds, were not the issue. I needed to focus on what I was achieving during those sacred moments.

This book places the focus squarely on purpose management because only by mastering your purpose can you maximize the impact you make each day.

My goal is to make you aware of your gift of 86400 seconds, and to manage your 86400 so that you live in your purpose, for your own benefit as well as for the benefit of others.

THE PAST WE CARRY

I've often found it interesting to watch vintage black-and-white TV programs that show old-fashioned traditions. One custom that I like in particular is the way a mother would measure her kids' heights on a wall. The children would stand, backs straight, heels pressed to the floor molding, as she took a pencil and slid it over the top of their heads to make a mark. They could see how much they'd grown. The tradition of marking a child's height is a visual way to show how time truly changes things.

I wish there were an equivalent way to measure one's growth into purpose. If only I could measure how my character is refined with the passing of time and how my heart and head are sharpened as one experience builds on top of another and then another. All are reflections of my true purpose, but the growth and the management of our purpose can never be measured by etchings on a wall. One of the greatest indicators of our soul's expansion into a life of purpose is how we choose to use our experiences and lessons as we move through the world.

"To live by grace means to acknowledge my whole life

story, the light side and the dark. In admitting my shadow side, I learn who I am and what God's grace means," Brennan Manning, a Franciscan priest and author, wrote in *The Ragamuffin Gospel: Good News for the Bedraggled, Beat-Up, and Burnt Out* (Multnomah Books, 1993).

So often we are scared of the whole story. We buy into the belief that because we once failed, we will always be failures or the belief that because we were once ashamed, we should always be ashamed. Our past—both the beauties and failures contained within it—is essential to our present. We would not be who we are without our heartaches, our scars, and moments of despair. In fact, we can choose to use the exact difficulties that once wounded us deeply to become better human beings.

Spiritualists from various faith traditions contend that trials and tribulations have a purpose: to help sharpen us. We tend to get comfortable and complacent when everything is going our way. At such moments we usually take our eyes off our goals and lose sight of our purpose. This is what happened to the children of Israel who were on a transgenerational quest to find the Promised Land.

One of the Adinkra symbols of the Ghanaian people depicts a bird that has its head turned around, craning its neck to take an egg off its back. The egg symbolizes knowledge gained in the past. The symbol as a whole embodies the principle that we can reach back for the knowledge of the past that will help build a foundation for the future.

I love this principle because it reflects the concept that to know where you're going, you must know where you've been. To live your life in alignment with your purpose, you must be willing to take the lessons, knowledge, and wisdom of the past with you on your journey. I also love the Sankofa imagery because the artist chose an egg, one of the most fragile items. You must be careful with an egg, or it will easily shatter and become a mess. The past is much the same. While it can serve as the most beneficial teacher, allowing us to grow, evolve, and stay true to our intended purpose, if we're not careful it can become the heaviest load, stunting our growth as human beings and derailing us from that very same purpose. We must respect the past and its lessons. We must also be careful not to depend completely on what has come before. It can be a burden rather than a blessing.

Your purpose is a fluid, organic force that can become distorted if you only view it looking backward. Living solely in the past can make you a prisoner of it and strip your present and future of its full potential.

The following three chapters address three primary principles for purpose management of your past: forgiveness, wisdom, and balance. The chapters provide you with a framework for incorporating these elements into your daily journey of a purpose-filled life. Each of these three characteristics is intimately linked to your past and your perception of it. By unleashing the power of forgiveness, wisdom, and balance, you will be better equipped to face situations and best use your 86400. The precious and valuable lessons from your past, both good and bad, can help you master your unique purpose.

1

Forgiveness: Yourself and Others

*To forgive is to set a prisoner free
and discover that the prisoner was you.*
—Lewis B. Smedes

Forgiveness allows us to be better purpose managers. Forgiveness allows us to let go of things that block our discovery of our purpose.

If you're at all like me, your greatest struggle, most likely, will be learning to forgive yourself, for the things you've done as well as for the things you haven't done.

I'm slowly forgiving myself for some things I believe I should have done for my father during years of illness before his death. For far too long and for far too many 86400s, I have chosen to carry a heavy burden of guilt regarding my father's death. As I'm compelled to write about this, to confess, I'm unsuccessfully holding back tears.

My father, Jimmie A. Red, died on October 5, 2008. He endured a number of health problems: heart failure, diabetes he developed later in life, and as a result both legs amputated in an effort to save him. It was not until the eleventh hour that I took his illness seriously, and by then it was too late to save him. I believe that if I had acted two, perhaps three, years sooner, many of his ailments could have been better managed.

My brother Greg was constantly warning me, "We have to do something. He's not taking care of himself." On some level, I did not believe him. My brother had been saying that for years, and my father was still here after having triple bypass surgery fifteen years previous. I always talked to my father in a joking way, not really getting serious enough to tell him he had to do better with his eating and overall health habits. My brother got so mad at me because of my nonchalant attitude regarding my father's health that he did not speak to me for a long time.

In my family, my schedule is probably the most flexible. I could have prepared my father's meals and spent more time getting him to understand that he must eat properly. I'm the queen of low-calorie healthy cooking in my family. I still don't understand why I didn't insist on doing more.

One day my father was looking ill and not feeling well. He fixed himself a plate of food, ignoring the no-salt dishes my mother prepared. He piled his plate high with mac and cheese and other things he shouldn't have been eating. Though I normally joked with him about such habits, that particular time, for some reason, I snapped. I stuck my bare hands right in the middle of his mac and cheese, grabbed it, and threw a great deal of it away. My father got so mad that he said a few choice words to me and refused to eat what was left. Perhaps if I had done more mac-and-cheese grabs he would have lived longer.

I could have done so much more, and I don't know why

I didn't. Losing him is so painful. I can't believe he is no longer here. I had the resources to get help, a psychologist, a nutritionist—something. However, I didn't.

The sicker he got, the more I didn't want to face it. I didn't want to think about it. I convinced myself that his sickness would pass with time. Instead, he passed. The hardest thing for me to do is forgive myself for not doing more, but I can't be productive with this weight. I have to move on. I'm not totally free from the "what could have and should have been," but each day I'm dedicated to lifting off the weight. Each new 86400, I grow more dedicated to refusing to spend my seconds worrying about the past.

I've given myself permission to forgive myself, right now, right here. I'm choosing to forgive me, so that I can face the pain of my loss. I can move forward to make the most of, not to waste, precious moments with the family that I still have. I'm not forgetting my past, but I'm choosing not to dwell on what I can't get back. I was given the blessing of time and experiences with my father, and I have the memory of all the seconds he gave to me and I to him. I have everything about him that was good, that made me who I am. I know in my heart that he would never blame me for what I did not do. I know he loved me, and I know he was proud of the woman I had become. I know that in order for him to continue to be proud of me, I can't stop. I can't let guilt and an inability to forgive myself continue to strangle me. I have the power to forgive myself, move forward, and use my time in a way that would make him proud, in a way that reflects my purpose.

We are all faulty. What is important is how we cope with our transgressions, failures, and flaws. As sinners who continually stumble, we need to stop pigeonholing ourselves in our past sin. Instead of letting past mistakes bury us in purposeless pursuits, let us realize we have a choice: to kneel at the feet of our sin or to drop-kick our sin in the face and do one of those phenomenally triumphant touchdown dances we witness on *Monday Night Football*.

We can conquer and move forward from our heart's greatest aches by forgiving ourselves and recognizing that Jesus spent far less time condemning than forgiving. He was clear about his purpose and used each of his 84600 seconds to the utmost. Jesus was on a mission to uplift and remind each of us that we are the salt of the earth and the light of the world. He did not harp on past misdeeds or present circumstances, but celebrated what could be, what everyone can become.

Focus your attention on your purpose, a task greatly assisted by your willingness to forgive yourself and others. View each new 86400 for what it is: a blessing and gift from God to continue on your journey to maximize your purpose. Understand and truly believe that U-turns on the road of life are always possible, even in what might seem to be unstoppable rush-hour traffic.

The Bible is explicit in Christ's hope for us and the battle He is willing to wage to bring us back from our ways to His kingdom. Consider Jesus in the garden of Gethsemane. His Disciples were surrounding Jesus when the soldiers came to arrest Him. When they said they were looking for Jesus of Nazareth, without hesitation, Jesus responded, "I told you that I am he.... If you are looking for me, then let these men go" (John 18:8).

Christ demonstrated an unthinkable dedication to us. He knew Judas had betrayed Him. He knew Peter would deny Him. He knew that all men would run to protect and care for themselves rather than stick their necks out for their Savior. It is for that very reason and our faults that Christ commits to us. Daily, on our behalf, He says, in effect, "Let them go." If we follow Him, He will love us unconditionally. He will save us.

Cleaning Agent

Forgiveness means to seek healing and cleanse self—to let go of hurts and grudges—so you can live free and unencumbered as God intended. You don't like to dwell on your negative aspects, your bad habits and characteristics, but you cling to them. Ridding yourself of them is essential. This cleansing of self-forgiveness is a necessary first step before you can arm yourself with positive and effective tools that will help you manage your purpose. If you were planning to attend a lavish dinner party and spent the first part of the day working in the garden and mowing the lawn, you wouldn't slip your fancy eveningwear right on over your dirt-covered body. You would first take a long, hot shower before you got decked out in your designer gown or tux. Cleanse your daily practices and life outlooks with life's most powerful cleaning agent: forgiveness.

Forgiveness is one of the most difficult tasks we'll tackle in our lives. Fear of confrontation and a lack of belief in God's providence lead us to ignore forgiveness; we pretend mercy isn't necessary in this world abounding with hurt and mistakes. We trick ourselves into believing that we *can't* forgive others or forgive ourselves. We believe that things we have done are *unforgivable* even though God says he has "rescued us from darkness and brought us into the kingdom of the Son he loves, in whom we have redemption, and the forgiveness of sins" (Colossians 1:14). We continually choose to believe mercy is inadequate.

Our lack of understanding about the power of forgiveness is a huge deterrent to managing our purpose, to living the life to which God has called us. When we choose to bypass forgiveness, we strip ourselves of so many essential elements of our future.

Think about it in terms of sickness and health. When we're not physically feeling well, we have to take steps to improve our well-being. One of those steps involves taking medicine. Most of us detest gulping down spoonfuls of cough syrup or swallowing pills, but it's often the medicine that heals our pounding headaches and aching bodies.

Forgiveness is the same antidote to our emotional sicknesses. Until we treat the hurts and pains in our lives, they will gnaw away at us. They will deprive us of a ripe present, wasting today's 86400: relationships with our family and friends, promotions at work, our drive to meet goals. We are stripped of our future hopes when we cling to our past wounds, wasting a significant portion of our hours, minutes, and seconds on the worst human activities—self-pity, guilt, bitterness, and anger. The result of becoming buddy-buddy with anger and resentment is an inflated image of self and a loss of life's true joys. Only through forgiveness can we heal hurts and move forward. We must learn to forgive others sincerely and forgive ourselves.

Emotional pain at its core derives from two primary sources: the people closest to us and ourselves.

When others wound us deeply, it is because they understand the nerve centers of our soul. They know how we tick. They've seen our buttons. They've witnessed our Achilles' heels, and they are tied, quite intimately, to the strings of our heart. What they say or do hurts all the more because of their proximity to our lives.

Friends will call me and ask if we can meet for coffee. They grab a dark roast and I sip my green tea while they tell me what has happened, perhaps how a close friend has wounded them deeply. "How could they possibly do this to me?" I can tell their hearts are truly bleeding. Later, I'll get the call again and, once more, sit across the table from them as they tell me a similar story and repeat the words, "How could they possibly do this to me?" I ask my friends, "Have you addressed the situation, have you confronted the individual?" Typically, they shake their heads and say, "I just don't know what to say to them." My friends are writhing in self-pity. They are playing the wounded victim and holding on, with severe passion, to how they've been wronged.

In the throes of victimhood, maximizing your 86400 is impossible because living your purpose is the farthest thing from your mind. Often we fail to forgive because we find a perverted empowerment in the victim role. We can claim the moral high ground and tell all who will listen to our sad story that we are right and the victimizer is wrong. We continue to suffer the pain of a broken and fractured relationship because we find it easier to claim victory in declaring "woe is me" than to confront the situation and find solutions.

The problems with this scenario are many. Foremost, when you choose victimization over forgiveness, you decide to remain chained to an unhealthy reality. Your time, energy, thoughts, and ideas are siphoned away from productive, purpose-focused activities. Potential and possibility are sacrificed to ego and fear. You give your all to a dying situation (victimization), rather than to your purpose.

I understand the peculiar power in playing the victim because I have done it so many times myself. We feel someone owes us a debt, but we are wrong.

We focus far too much on what others say and do, and far too little on our own actions and words. It creates an unbalanced, unhealthy perspective that skews our point of view. Matthew 7:3 says, "Why do you look at the speck of sawdust in your brother's eye and pay no attention to the plank in your own eye?" When we stop seeing ourselves as victims, we look at the situation and realize our own participation in the wrong or understand that we could make the same mistake, and it becomes possible for us to forgive the other person.

When we cling to our anger toward others, we miss life's true purpose. Our anger consumes us. It demands our thoughts, our time, and our hearts. If we give all our time and energy to anger, we miss the precious opportunities to invest it in our real treasures: our families, our passions, our callings, all those things that reflect our God-intended purpose.

Think of all the energy you're investing in your anger and pity. Now visualize how you can invest that energy into your passion, potential, purpose. Forgiveness frees you to truly be yourself and make your 86400s purposeful and joy filled.

A common misconception about forgiveness is that its power and intent is for the person being forgiven. But forgiveness is for the forgiver. How many times have you held on to a grudge against someone, and while you have been stewing in your anger, that person has been living life to the fullest, oblivious to your sullen state? Most of the persons you feel have offended you are unaware that they did anything you thought was harmful or egregious. Even if they are aware of your pain, they may not care. Your hurt, anger, frustration, depression, and raised blood pressure have little or no effect on the person with whom you are angry, but that anger has a devastating effect on you.

FORGIVENESS

I live right next to Lakewood Church in Houston, Texas. My husband and I are members there. Marcos Witt steps in for Joel Osteen from time to time throughout the year. It is always a delight to hear Marcos Witt preach. I had the pleasure of hearing one of his sermons that touched on forgiveness not too long ago, so I asked him to share some of his thoughts on forgiveness with me.

Marcos Witt

Associate pastor for the Hispanic congregation of Lakewood Church in Houston, Texas, Latin Grammy Award–winning composer and singer, founder of CanZion Institute, an international school for worship leaders and music ministers and author of inspirational books.

Forgiveness is a characteristic that requires us to give. I read a book one time that said forgiving is the key to everything. The premise was that when you forgive, you are releasing yourself to a greater cause. The book also talked about forgiveness as another part of giving. I think that when you give to someone your forgiveness that's a great act of not only selflessness, but also it's a great act of kindness and mercy. The Bible always encourages us to forgive others. It is important as a personal value to constantly live with the mentality of forgiving, but, unfortunately, it seems to be a value that is becoming scarce. When you forgive, it literally frees you from the bondage of the hurt and the pain. When you forgive, you don't have to seek revenge or vengeance. You don't have to try to balance the scales. Forgiveness really releases us from all that. Forgiveness is freedom, and with freedom, you are better able to manage your day, to make the most of your 86400.

By being a forgiving person, I'm free to concentrate on the things that really matter. I think that people who are unforgiving allow bitterness to come in, and bitterness paralyzes you. When you are paralyzed, what can you do? Not much, right? So being able to forgive is so important. With forgiveness in your heart, you don't have to waste any of your precious 86400 on things like anger, hurt, revenge. Forgiveness allows me to be free to manage my day doing things that are productive.

Your 86400 is given to you once, and then it is gone. It is important to decide what you are going to do with that 86400. We are today the results of our decisions from yesterday. So it is important to be conscious of what we are doing with the time we have today, because it will affect tomorrow.

As a businessman, entrepreneur, pastor, communicator, and a leader, all kinds of things come up in my day. On top of that, I have the honor of being a dad, a father-in-law, a grandpa. My day involves time listening to and talking to the Lord. It involves meetings, some days more than others. During the course of my day, I always look at world headlines, especially Latin American headlines, because that's an area that I move in quite a lot. My day involves perusing my e-mail and, these days, Facebook, Twitter, and stuff like that. It involves leadership decisions, questions asked of me by my team. I have 800-plus people working for me full time somewhere in Latin America or around the world. I have CEOs from some of the divisions of the companies I have started who call me or send me e-mails dealing with some of the larger issues.

Every now and then, I get to do really fun stuff like being invited to the White House or special events. About ten times a year, I get to step in for Pastor Joel Osteen and speak to the entire congregation at Lakewood Church. My life is full of challenges, excitement, fun, and work. I do enjoy what I do; I never feel as if I'm working. John Maxwell, the leadership expert and author, said if you like what you do, you will never work again in your life. I love my job as ambassador of the kingdom of God to Latin America.

What has been most beneficial to me in becoming successful is always being conscious of the fact that everything I have is a gift from God. When you start off in life with that understanding, then you will walk forward with great confidence. The gift of music that I have is a gift from God, the gift of communication is a gift from God, the gift of relationship is a gift from God. Having God as the center of my life and letting everything else revolve around that has brought me success.

You know, the definition of success is different from one person to the other. I heard a definition of success years ago that I really identify with. The person said, "Success is being loved more by those who know you best." That's powerful. By that benchmark, I'm successful. I've always placed God first in my life and walked in relationship with Him. He has led me down paths of goodness, blessings, and mercy.

Another tool that has helped me to be successful is doing the will of God with my life. When you understand what the will of God is for your life, and you walk in that, you will be successful. If His will for you means you never sing or grace the cover of a magazine, as long as you are doing God's will with your life, you will be happy, content, and successful at it, because you are doing what he created you to do.

Claiming Your Identity

This Christmas, my friend went to a candlelight service at a local church. The sanctuary was old, and its roof was undergoing construction. When she pulled into the parking lot, the work on the church was visible. Scaffolding surrounded the church on all sides, and the shiny, copper piping had been plucked from the structure and set visibly aside for recycling. She thought nothing of it as she parked, walked inside, and took her seat in the candlelit pews.

Much to her surprise, that night the preacher didn't tell a story about Jesus' birth, but rather about the copper. The old piping would secure roughly $5,000, a none-too-small sum, particularly during a season when the congregation's ability to give had dwindled. However, a week before Christmas, the pastor had come to the church to find the copper stolen from the premises. The thief left a number of tracks, and within a few days the copper was returned to the church and the man who had stolen it was read his rights, charged, and released on bond.

Desperate not to face a trial and conviction, the thief came to the church and begged for lenience from the pastor. He apologized for his actions and asked for mercy. Seeing the man's genuine repentance, the pastor forgave him and didn't press charges. But before letting him go on his way, he insisted on a point. "When you drive by this church from now on," he said, "remember not that you are guilty, but that you are forgiven." The pastor reminded the man that how we choose to identify ourselves in situations is an essential component in leading a better life. We are forgiven. We are not guilty. We are new creations.

My friend's tale touched me deeply, especially since I was wrestling with my own issues of guilt about my failure to do more for my father before I forgave myself as the thief was forgiven. So often in life, we, like the thief, are haunted by daily reminders of our past transgressions, the mistakes we've made or the things we should have done. But dwelling in guilt and shame is certain to halt personal growth because it saps energy for the pursuit of our purpose. If we take refuge in our failures, the world is a still, somber place. When we choose to forgive, we discover new opportunities to succeed.

I am reminded of the Robert De Niro movie *The Mission*. In it De Niro played an eighteenth-century slaver whose lavish lifestyle was paid for by the pain of the South American Indians he kidnapped and sold into slavery. De Niro's most beloved relative was his brother, but De Niro's character discovered that his wife was sleeping with his brother. The character ended up killing his brother by duel, viewed as justified during that time. De Niro had the opportunity to go on living his life as a free man. However, he became a victim of his own guilt over killing his brother. Distraught, De Niro's character chose to stay locked up in a cell, refusing food or water because he felt unworthy of life.

As long as the man held on to his unforgiveness, he had no time or energy for productive pursuits. A priest offered a way out: penance. De Niro's character chose to carry the heavy armor he used for kidnapping up steep, treacherous mountains and give it to the very people he spent his life enslaving. Only after he completed his trek, presented the armor to them, and offered himself in their service was he able to forgive himself. However, to his surprise, moved by his actions, the people the man once enslaved forgave him. He then dedicated the rest of his life to protecting the people from others who sought to rob them of their freedom. He was able to live a worthy and powerful purpose. Forgiveness is the beginning of our management of our purpose. Forgiveness frees us to focus not on what once was, but on what can be, what we can do right now to make that future a reality. The Lord takes our transgressions, acknowledges them, and cancels the debt. Then He does an amazing thing: He forgets them. He proceeds to love us, care for us, and intercede for us as though we were always clean, blameless, and loyal. But He doesn't stop there. He takes our life, puts it in the palm of His hand, and begins to mold us toward His purpose for us. He aims to give us a future that separates us from the pain and sin of our past. Titus 3:3–5 says, "At one time we were foolish, disobedient, deceived and enslaved by all kinds of passions and pleasures. We lived in malice and envy, being hated and hating one another. But when the kindness and love of God our Savior appeared, he saved us, not because of righteous things we had done, but because of his mercy."

We are in the grip of His mercy and fully aware of the power of forgiveness. Because of this, the seconds, minutes, hours, and days before us hold more potential than we ever allowed ourselves to believe. God has placed divine purpose within each of us. It is our responsibility to live it, share it, master it, and celebrate it.

86400 Adviser: Pastor Rudy Rasmus— Forgiveness

A few years ago, the Reverend Rudy Rasmus of Houston, Texas, found his own faith tested. He had discovered that his daughter, who was then eighteen years old, had been molested by a family member when she was four. Not only could he not forgive the offender, he was not even willing to preach about forgiveness, one of the most fundamental teachings of Jesus.

Just learning about the transgression "put me in such a difficult position," he said.

"On one hand, as a pastor, I'm responsible for the faith development of a group of people and the Bible is explicitly clear about forgiveness. One of my responsibilities is to encourage people to practice forgiveness. During that time, it became virtually impossible for me to talk about forgiveness because I wasn't willing to do it."

With his wife, Juanita, Rasmus co-pastors one of Houston's most dynamic and life-changing fellowships, St. John's United Methodist Church. He is an emergent messenger, an urban prophet and global humanitarian with a passion for outreach to our world's poorest citizens. Beginning with nine members in 1992, his church, known to many as St. John's Downtown, has grown to more than 9000 members (3000 of them homeless or formerly homeless) in sixteen years. It is one of the most culturally diverse congregations in the country, where every week people of every social and economic background share the same pew.

Its shepherd has preached and written about ministering to the wounded. Now, this powerful preacher and compassionate minister was in need of healing. As his feelings about the violation of his daughter ricocheted from "homicidal tendencies to deep feelings of remorse and guilt for allowing it to happen," the preacher who was a beacon for so many began to see a therapist. He said the counselor "began to help me appropriate the action; to put the action in perspective with the goal of moving forward.

"So you ask me, 'What is forgiveness?'" he told me. "Forgiveness is the act of moving forward.

"I'm in the business where the icon, the founder of this business (God), tells folk all the time that it is most advantageous to forgive," the minister said. "How can you be forgiven unless you forgive? The icon of this faith (God) has repeated concepts around the need for forgiveness. But I have found that process and that practice difficult when it is time to do it."

The pastor is a firm believer in the power of forgiveness in helping people better manage their 86400. He knows from personal experience that forgiveness will free you up to live your purpose once again.

Failure to forgive, Reverend Rasmus told me, would be like going through my 86400 with the offending person on my back. Visualizing this, I could feel myself being weighed down and unable to do those things near and dear to me. I could feel myself being blocked from living my purpose.

"And we wonder why we are tired and can't sleep," he said. "Imagine going to sleep with four people on your back. First off, you can't find a comfortable position. Imagine just trying to move through your day with people on your back. So forgiveness is moving forward without the encumbrances of the person, offense, or deed or act as a part of your being, your spirit. When we forgive, we are saying to the people on our back, 'No longer can you ride into the future with me. No longer will I carry you into another day. I'm going to release you right now.'

"When you get those folk off your back, you become far more productive," preached the preacher extraordinaire. The sheer fact of not having that human being riding with you into your future means that your load is lighter. A lighter load is representative of a brighter future—more time to do what you got to do, more ways to use that 86400 seconds."

To forgive does not mean we must forget, as so many people might think. "I believe that you should forgive and remember to keep from repeating the same scenario—committing the act to memory that needs forgiveness, committing the person to memory," said Pastor Rasmus.

When he released the person who committed the offense against his family, his load lightened and his soul lit up.

"In that situation with my daughter, from the time I released that person, the light began to come back on in my own spirit," he recalled. "I had turned the light out."

His willingness to forgive was even tested one day when, he said, "that creep walked out in front of me" at a crosswalk while the pastor was driving to meet some people for lunch.

"That was a test," he concluded. "I'm at the corner, and I'm thinking, 'Hmmm.' But you know my Facebook status that day read, 'I've passed the supreme test, and unconditional love won.'"

Vengeance is not compatible with forgiveness. Unconditional love must keep winning over our spirits.

"Does it mean that the person is no longer a creep?" asks Reverend Rasmus. "Heck, no! Does it mean that that person won't commit the offense again if given the opportunity? Absolutely not! That person is a creep and will do it again. You are not responsible for that person's next 86400. You are responsible for yours."

To keep running through your 86400 without encumbrance, without the weight of others on your back, you have to leave behind the burden of an unforgiving spirit.

Rasmus believes being conscious of your 86400 frees you from the bondage of past mistakes and future worries so that you can manage your purpose.

"Forgiveness is the most difficult concept in the human condition," the minister said. "It requires you to prioritize memory, to be selective in appropriating drama."

His candor made the concept of forgiveness and how it relates to purpose come alive. "We only have the moments, the seconds in front of us," the pastor said. "You know I can't do anything about the moments that have passed, but my 86400 in front of me are for me to govern, and those are the most important."

What he does to ensure that his purpose is being lived is to define daily victory for himself. "When I wake up every day, my question to God is, Who are we going to help today? And before I finish my day, it is a successful day if somebody got helped. It is important that you define victory for yourself, or else you will never be finished; you will never get anything done." Forgiveness is a powerful tool to enable us to let go of things that impede progress and keep us from moving forward toward our purpose.

"Something that I have learned in the midst of trauma and trials is the importance of living in the absolute moment," Pastor Rasmus said. "I can't even live in the week ahead, but I can be the most effective me right now. I can be the most loving me right now. I can be the most passionate and compassionate me right now, and the mistakes I've made prior to that, I can't do anything about those either. So my advice to folk that are struggling is to value the moment you are in right now. Your 'right now' controls your future."

The growth of St. John's was possible because its pastor is amazingly clear about his purpose. He attributes the success of the church to a compassionate congregation that shares his purpose and vision of tearing down the walls of classism, sexism, and racism and building bridges of unconditional love, universal recovery, and unprecedented hope. Rasmus also co-founded Bread of Life, Inc., a not-for-profit corporation that provides more than 7000 hot meals each month to homeless men and women.

Although I had heard of "Pastor Rudy" over the years, I was formally introduced to him by my friend Councilwoman Ada Edwards, who told me St. John's was so awesome that I just had to come worship with her one Sunday. I agreed, knowing that something really special must be going on at St. John's to get my friend to attend both the 8 a.m. and the 10 a.m. services practically every Sunday.

After visiting and getting to know Pastor Rasmus, I, too, decided to get involved at St. John's and to share my passion for literature through a book club for individuals that its homeless ministry serves. I am not a member at St. John's, but I attend services there about once a month.

The minister's example of overcoming and forgiving is a daily reminder that the way to let my light shine is to release all negative baggage by forgiving myself and others. Then, and only then, can I truly live my purpose. I can remember these words from the pastor: "At the end of the day, when I love someone, regardless of what he has done to me or mine, I am released to love not only that person but everyone else in my path. With that comes an incredible and amazing freedom."

Your Next 600 Seconds

Devote your next 600 seconds to understanding how forgiveness can help you make the most of your God-given time by living your purpose. Think of someone you have not been able to forgive. Can you forgive that person at this moment? Right here. Right now. If you can do so, tell that person as soon as you can of your decision to forgive. If you can't forgive now, pray for the ability to forgive this person. Is there something for which you have been unable to forgive yourself? Tell yourself now that you forgive you. Use these ten minutes to discover how you can move from thought to the act of forgiving. Reflect. Evaluate. Plan. Act. Remember: It is your time, and you have the power to make the most of it.

Seconds for the Spirit

> *"And when you stand praying, if you hold anything against anyone, forgive him, so that your Father in heaven may forgive you your sins" (Mark 11:25).*

2

Wisdom:
The Act of Doing

*A good traveler has no fixed plans
and is not intent on arriving.*
—Laozi

Ever since I got my first skateboard in the fourth grade—
a long, thick, plastic, bright pink board—I have loved the
sport of skateboarding. I still get away to skate parks whenever I have a free moment. I spent much of my early childhood at my grandmother's house while my parents were in
school working on their advanced degrees. So I would often
ask my grandmother if I could go down the hill and skateboard with my friends. The answer was always no. I would
beg and plead, but the answer would still be no. She would
repeat a long monologue about how dangerous it was and
how kids were breaking bones and being hit by cars.

"Right out here in front of the house is plenty enough
room for you to play on that contraption," she would say.
"Every time you get on that contraption you end up with
scrapes and bruises."

Trying hard not to laugh, she would add, "I have a good mind to make you just jump up and down in the house and fall down where I can see you," she would say.

As she did after saying no to many of my dangerous requests, she would often end by saying, "You will understand when you get older. Experience is a good teacher."

She was right in not letting me go out unsupervised to skateboard in a dangerous place. What my grandmother said made no sense to me at the time. The consequences associated with skateboarding down a steep hill had no meaning to me. I lacked her wisdom. Over time and through many experiences, my wisdom has matured. Having wisdom goes beyond an accumulated learning that keeps us out of danger. Wisdom is knowing what to do, why you should do it, and, finally, getting busy doing the darn thing. Contrary to popular belief and even most definitions, *wisdom* is an action word. Though it's not a verb, wisdom is all about action. Wisdom not only guides purposeful actions, wisdom makes your intentions take shape as tangible acts. Wisdom is one of the most concrete of the purpose characteristics.

While we often think of wisdom in relation to scholarly, academic, or professional pursuits, wisdom of self is essential. Wisdom is a refined understanding of who we are, what we desire, and what our strengths and weaknesses are. With wisdom of self, we are able to move intentionally and effectively toward our life's goals—making better use of our time, talent, and resources. With wisdom, we discern our purpose and choose paths that allow us to better manage and magnify it. Without wisdom, we sabotage our own efforts and waste precious seconds and days wondering why our actions bear no fruit.

Picture this. It's the day of a race. A string of men hovers at the starting line. Shorts. Running shoes. School jerseys. They all look the same except one young man, perhaps in his late teens. He has a long, graceful body with sculpted arms and legs that are lean like a cheetah's. Bending, breaking, and stretching toward the ground with strong movements, the young man has a focused glint in his eyes, as though he's picturing something vividly—probably his impending victory with bulbs flashing, hands clapping, and the roar of the appreciative crowd. Whatever it is he sees, you know he's there, fully present, and soaking up the moment. He's ready to run.

Looking at him, we'd all assume the same thing. The man is a born runner. We'd take him a-million-to-one over Slow Poke Sammy with the short, stubby legs who is standing at the end of the lineup in his hand-me-down running shoes. Yet we'd all be operating under the same unfounded assumption: The youth who caught our eye looks the part. He acts the part, but before his body starts moving, how can we ever really know if he *fills* the part?

The gun fires, the race begins, and the young man's feet, left after right, are hitting the hot pavement. One mile quickly turns into two, and he looks unfazed. When mile three hits, you can tell something isn't quite right. His right hand grips his abdomen. His breathing, once even, becomes heavy panting. Mile four comes, and the man no longer looks the Olympian he did at the starting line. It's all he can do to keep stride. As much as he looks the part, he is unprepared. Untrained.

Though few of us are willing to admit it, this man pursued his race the way most of us pursue our lives. We have good intentions. We have high goals. We are outfitted with the necessary equipment. *We look the part.* Yet, somewhere along the way, we have forgotten the most essential component for our success: our training.

We approach our goals but we aren't thoroughly prepared. While we are full of heart, gumption, and stamina, we lack understanding. We lack wisdom.

As a youngster, when I would hear the word *wisdom*, the first word I thought of was *old*. The second word I thought of was *gray*. I pictured someone like Gandalf from the film *The Lord of the Rings* hovering over society with an excessively long beard and an over-whittled cane. But wisdom isn't an attribute of age. It's something that comes as a result of experience, and it is an essential part of our training to make the most of our 86400. The people who are willing to open their eyes, their ears—all of their senses—and take in the world will be much more equipped to address life's situations than those who remain blind and deaf to reality, pressing forward with their naivete, insistent that they "know enough." For the runner, looking the part couldn't win the race. To cross the finish line, he needed to train adequately. He needed to develop a mental and physical toughness that could withstand and conquer the road ahead.

All of us, like the runner, need training. We need to prepare our hearts and minds with an arsenal of intellect for the treacherous, winding, and often surprising road ahead. Proverbs 20:5 says, "The purposes of a man's heart are deep waters, but a man of understanding draws them out." The biggest question isn't whether you need it, but how you get it, suggests author John Eldredge in *Wild at Heart: Discovering the Secret of a Man's Soul* (Thomas Nelson, 2001). The wisdom of understanding—which entails patience, forethought, experience, and grace—can often be the greatest weapon you have.

WISDOM

A friend told me about VolunteerMatch, a popular Web site (www.volunteermatch.org) of a nonprofit organization that connects people who want to serve with the causes and organizations that need their time. I managed to reach VolunteerMatch's president, Greg Baldwin, by phone. It was a delight to find how eager he was to speak about volunteerism. We talked about how wisdom, purpose, and service relate to making the best use of our 86400.

Greg Baldwin

President of VolunteerMatch since 1998; former sales executive with the Leo Burnett advertising agency and co-founder of 2d Interactive, Inc., a Boston-based technology start-up; and board chair of the Council for Certification in Volunteer Administration.

I've been volunteering since I was seven or eight. I find that this is a part of my purpose. I believe I was born with an inborn urge to be helpful. When I'm not being helpful, I really feel different about myself. Being helpful is a piece of my life that I feel is really important to make the time for. For as long as I can remember, being helpful is what makes me tick, what makes me happy and satisfied and feel like I'm doing what I can as a person to be all that I can be.

I think most people don't understand how rewarding, fulfilling, and satisfying it can be to make volunteering a part of their lives. I acknowledge and appreciate the incredible desire that each of us has to give back. For me the wisdom is that I believe people want to give back; finding the opportunity to give back or make the time to give back is what stops most people. Volunteering is rewarding and fulfilling in ways you could not imagine.

I really think that people who have not tried it are missing out on something they will find personally, emotionally, and socially very satisfying.

However, I believe it is wise to give other people the benefit of the doubt—that they are not just in it for themselves and that if you approach situations believing or having a faith that they have interest, that will extend beyond their own selfish self-interest. It's a framework that has allowed people to give back above and beyond, as opposed to (treating) them as if they were selfish to began with. There is some wisdom in not viewing people as single-mindedly self-interested, but to understand that a lot of different things motivate people and that people are more complicated than just being selfish—seeing people as more complicated than just seeing their own interest. People are also motivated by the satisfaction of being helpful. Their own fulfillment requires them to find something to contribute that someone else can appreciate. This is a huge motivator.

One example is the car pool I take to work. I love the fact that every day my day begins with a ride from a complete stranger. I cross the bridge to the San Francisco Bay Area. It is a casual car pool. I basically hitchhike to work every day—which is neat, people organizing themselves to help themselves. It is not an organized car pool or an official one. No fee or membership, just people working together for the last ten years. I just walk to the car pool and wait in line. It's in North Berkeley. Cars pull up, and I regularly get in the car with another stranger and a driver I've never met. We all go across the bridge together, and we get to use the car-pool lane. They drop me off in San Francisco, and I walk the rest of the way to work. It is very satisfying.

The thing that has been most beneficial to my success was having the wisdom to quit my first job. I graduated with a public service degree from Brown University. Not quite knowing what to do with it, I got a job in advertising. I spent two fast-paced, fun-filled years in the ad business but was really unfulfilled. Some soul searching and wisdom gave me the courage to quit. I spent a year with a friend on the beach in Cape Cod, reading and telling our parents that we were writing the great American novel, but we were really trying to figure out what we were going to do with the rest of our lives. The experience on the beach really put things in perspective. I read all those classic books that I was supposed to read in college but never had the chance. Books by William James, Emerson, Thoreau, and those other great classics helped me find what was important to me. I guess in fancy talk, I was looking for myself, my worldview, and I found it hanging at the beach in Cape Cod.

I came out of that experience believing that whatever I decided to do, I had to be honest with myself as to whether or not I was interested in it or just faking it. I made a promise to myself that I would not ever fake it, that I would be honest that what I was getting out of a job was what I really needed to get. That has landed me in a place like this, such a good fit with what I enjoy and what is fulfilling to me, my personal interest, my interest in commitment, in technology, and in service.

I've come to see that the act of consumption, consumption, and consumption as a strategy for happiness and success was definitely not the strategy for me. It just did not make sense to me. It did not make me happy having lots and lots of stuff. I had some notion early on that what I wanted in my job was the ability to make a contribution. I felt that other people were also looking for that same kind of satisfaction in their lives. There is something enormously satisfying about making a contribution and getting back appreciation.

We really created VolunteerMatch for people to be able to find out what was out there so that they could make it a part of their time. Just doing it when someone asks makes it harder to fit it into your schedule. We thought it would be great if people could see the thousands of opportunities out there so they could find a good match for them. Matching their passion and schedules. Our mission is to make it easier for good people and good causes to connect. We want to create a world where more people are able to find a meaningful opportunity to give back.

A key insight that led us to build VolunteerMatch was that more people would help out if they understood their choices. Another piece of wisdom I want to share with people is to spend some time looking around, use services like ours and others to look at your volunteer options. Even in a tough economy, service and volunteering keeps you active and engaged. It looks great on a resume, makes it easier to get a job. It looks better when you have something going on than when you have nothing going on.

You have to make time for things that are important. We are lucky in my office because we have office policy that allows us to volunteer one day a month. I will chip in on just about any cause if I can find the time. But I do find that I most like problem solving. I like troubleshooting. I was a volunteer at the Museum of Science in Boston. I basically was the computer IT support—and therapist. I would go around the building helping staff with their broken computers. I loved the Museum of Science as a kid, so to come in and help the people who ran it with their computer problems was what I loved. I also found that I really enjoyed volunteering as a Big Brother. I found that to be really challenging but also fulfilling and rewarding as well, and eye opening. My wife and I spend a lot of time volunteering at our daughters' school. That's something that is important to us. Finding the time is the issue.

I always make an effort to include volunteering as a part of my schedule. The last piece of wisdom I'd like to share is to tell people to be fussy; look until you find something you really do care about.

Who You Are and Whose You Are

Imagine you were visiting a new state for the first time, say South Dakota. On the first day, you visited the national parks and somehow got lost on the roads trying to get back to your cabin. It's completely dark outside, you don't see any road signs, and you have no idea where you are. At that point, even if a magic map floated down from Heaven with a big, red X marking your cabin's exact location, it wouldn't matter. *You wouldn't be able to get to your destination because you can't identify your present location.* It's the same in life. Before you start moving and making any progress, you have to know where you are. You can start heading in the right direction when wisdom comes into play. One of the greatest roadblocks to action, initiative, and productivity is a lack of personal understanding and self-evaluation.

Wisdom is accumulated learning, the ability to discern inner qualities and relationships. Wisdom is insight, good sense, and judgment. This accumulated learning is essential in all facets of life because its pursuit allows you to know yourself better and understand who you are, what you desire, where you are strong, as well as where you need growth. This wisdom of self provides you with a clarity of purpose that translates into an ability to get more out of each 86400. You are better able to live a life of intention and relevance, and to make a difference.

The often-quoted ancient Greek admonition to "know thyself" is one of the greatest commands we have. It is something Socrates, one of the most influential thinkers in the Western world, believed in deeply. The Socratic method of examining and questioning in order to discover the truth has become a cornerstone of our scientific process. The first part of the scientific process is creating a hypothesis, a proposed explanation for why something happens. From there, a series of questions is asked that whittles away at the assumption to discover the truth. When Socrates modeled this method, he wasn't thinking about science or medicine; he was thinking about people. "I know you won't believe me," he said, as quoted in an online article titled "Socrates" by Philip Coppens, an author and investigative journalist, "but the highest form of human excellence is to question oneself and others."

Part of my journey of finding out who I really am and what I'm here for began when a friend invited me to his church. Arriving early, I ventured into the church bookstore to browse until my friend arrived. The bookstore was a natural attraction to me as I love to read and I am always looking for a good book. Still, it had been some time since I had visited a church bookstore or the spiritual section in any bookstore. I attended and graduated from a Catholic high school. I must thank my parents for putting me in a religious grade school. It gave me a strong foundation in morality and character and a relationship with God. As an adult, however, I had strayed away from a personal relationship with God.

That day in the bookstore, *The One Year Bible* (Tyndale House, 1986) caught my attention. It is laid out to give you a very workable routine for reading the Bible in one year. I bought *The One Year Bible* and took it on as a challenge. I said, "One year? Ha, ha. I bet I can read this in three to six months." This challenge, just another task, put me on a path to discover my purpose.

I had read the Bible in parts throughout grade school

and here and there as an adult, but never as a book that I would pick up like a novel and just read. As I began to race through it, I found myself slowing down. I discovered that after reading several passages, I was unable to pull out and fully grasp one cohesive thought. I was missing the point. I slowed down and began to read for understanding. I became curious about the Bible. It brought back memories of some of the lessons the nuns taught me in grade school. It helped me to solve problems I encountered. It lifted my spirits. It even made me angry at times. Reading passages from Romans, Jeremiah, Matthew, and other books prompted me to look at my past. I pulled out some of my old religion tests from grade school. (Yes, I still have some of my work from as far back as first grade.) I began to look at me, question just what I was doing with my life, and wonder aloud exactly why I was here. *The One Year Bible* was the beginning of my quest to seek purpose. Not only did reading the Bible allow me to understand better who I am, but the act of reading it, seeking spiritual instruction, was a wise choice. I began to practice the knowledge and understanding I gained by reading Scripture. Knowing and doing are two different things. To quote evangelist Paula White, "Doing is an act of wisdom." My act of "doing" *The One Year Bible* gave me a much clearer picture of Lavaille.

God commanded us to evaluate deeply who we are, and to look past the surface of everyday actions and conversations to see who He had originally created us to be. Romans 12:2 reads, "Do not conform any longer to the pattern of this world, but be transformed by *the renewing of your mind.* Then you will be able to test and approve what God's will is—his good, pleasing and perfect will."

Throughout Scripture, we receive reminders that we are

far more than what we assume ourselves to be. Jeremiah 1:5 says, "Before I formed you in the womb I knew you, before you were born I set you apart; I appointed you as a prophet to the nations." I knew you before I formed you in your mother's womb? Likewise, Jesus says in Matthew 5:13–14, "You are the salt of the earth. . . . You are the light of the world."

Pursuit of who God intends for us to be gives us the wisdom necessary to tap into our passions and mesh them with the concerns of the world. With wisdom, we are empowered to maximize our purpose and make life better for ourselves and others.

In Job, the book of trials, you see clearly how God calls us to look beyond our pain and beyond our circumstance to discern carefully our Lord's intentions for our life. "Hear my words, you wise men; listen to me, you men of learning. For the ear tests words as the tongue tastes food. Let us discern for ourselves what is right; let us learn together what is good" (Job 34:2–4).

When you seek to "know thyself," it's not simply knowing *who* you are, but *whose* you are. You are God's child; you are the Almighty's precious and beloved son or daughter. This is wisdom; it will always be a point of strength and power.

Proverbs 9:10–11 says, "The fear of the Lord is the beginning of wisdom, and knowledge of the Holy One is understanding. For through me your days will be many, and years will be added to your life. If you are wise, your wisdom will reward you."

It's essential to take a discerning look at our own life, and it's just as important that we remain cognizant of *whose* we are. When we are in awe and reverence of who our Creator truly is, we understand that we are protected and blessed by a mighty higher power. We are able to recognize that we come from, are surrounded by, live in, and have access to an unlimited source of power, creativity, protection, and strength. Knowledge that we belong to the Holy One truly is understanding. This knowledge gives us the strength to move confidently through life, discerning our calling, ultimately helping us make the most of our God-given 86400.

Reap the Harvest

Wisdom is valuable in making our daily decisions. It equips us to make the best choices, especially the hard ones.

While wisdom is, in large part, an accumulated blessing— something that develops with time and experience—it is something, too, that we can prod along. God gave us the greatest daily resource we could ask for when he gave us the Bible. It covers just about every subject we could imagine. Even in today's changing world, it remains markedly relevant, pointing us to salvation. We have to ask ourselves this hard question: Why don't we daily invest time in reading it, understanding it? My rediscovery of self started with *The One Year Bible*, but my living in purpose is sustained by my daily reading of the Bible.

Say you were an attorney preparing to litigate an important case. Would you go into the courtroom the day of the trial not having thoroughly researched your client's evidence and story? Would you have neglected to research the opposing side's point of view and evidence? Just as the attorney must prepare for his trial, you prepare for your everyday life when you read and study the Bible. Is there a better example as to how we should live than Jesus? Is there a better resource for discovering how to have a fulfilling, rewarding 86400 than the Bible? For centuries, our guide to greater living has been in print, continually at our fingertips. The stories and lessons are always there for us to harvest and apply to our own situations. From having a healthy marriage to coping with an argument with a friend, we can crack the spine of the Good Book for truth and wisdom.

As you persist in your search for and development of wisdom, personal understanding, and spiritual growth, make daily Bible reading a part of your routine. It will stretch your imagination, heighten your understanding, and deepen your beliefs and hopes. It is the most important key to wisdom.

86400 Adviser: Paula White—Wisdom

Paula White refers to herself as a "messed-up Mississippi girl" who transformed her life of tragedy and poverty into a model of triumph, prosperity, and purpose. Wisdom made the difference in her life, allowing her to put her tortured past behind and reach out to heal others.

"I was lying in a very dark place, experientially," she said. "Then the wisdom of God was saying, 'Praise me in the midst of the mess. Praise me anyhow. Not praise me for it, but praise me in it.' What are you grateful for? Find an attitude of gratitude. Suddenly, through the wisdom of God and obeying his ways and his words and applying it, my darkness began to turn into daylight."

Today she is a minister, author, TV personality, and mother who has dedicated her life to helping others transform their circumstances and discover God's unique purpose for their lives. For Pastor White, the journey began in the small town of Tupelo, Mississippi, where her seemingly normal family life was turned upside down by her father's suicide when she was five years old. In the years that followed, she suffered abuse and struggled through her pain until she developed a relationship with Jesus Christ in her late teens. Eventually she began to minister to others in the urban cores of Washington, D.C., Los Angeles, and, later, Tampa, Florida, where she co-founded Without Walls International Church.

"I live life from the inside out, and I would tell anyone who is lost or struggling that it is never too late," she said, "that today is a brand-new day. That this is your moment: seize it. For people who are lost and struggling I completely understand. I was not always on this pathway of wholeness and balance."

She tells the suffering, "No matter where you are right now, with wisdom, which is more than just a decision, but taking these tools that are being given to you in this book and applying them in your life, you will have transformation power, and you are going to look different in a year from now. The landscape of your life will change."

White explained that wisdom is not the same as knowledge or even understanding. "The Bible clearly shows us that there is knowledge, understanding, and wisdom," she said. "Knowledge is the accumulation of facts; taking in the word of God and literally knowing from instruction. Understanding refers to our ability to arrange those facts. It has to do with insight, discernment, and discretion: union by association, or to grasp, to put together—knowledge acquired, obtained, and extended.

"Thus, knowledge is the accumulation of facts. Understanding is the arrangement of those facts, but wisdom is the application of those facts," added White. "If there are five frogs on a wall and one decides to jump off, how many frogs are on the wall? All five, because deciding is not doing. So wisdom is not a decision, it is the actual doing of it. Without wisdom, which is the application of knowledge and understanding, we don't actually see production in our life."

Nor can we effectively use our 86400 to fulfill our purpose.

"When I apply insight into my life," the minister continued, "I realize that I am not limited and locked into this 86400 seconds or 24 hours. With that mind-set, there is always more to do and not enough time to do it. However, by the wisdom of God I can be efficient and highly effective in life because I can fully engage. I can produce as I was created to produce."

Unlike God, time is unforgiving. "We can't get any more time in a day," she said. "But when we manage what is endlessly available to us, our energy within, that's the key. Then I'm not managing time, I'm using time."

I saw Paula White for the first time at one of my visits with Michael Jackson at his Neverland Ranch many years ago. On that particular occasion Michael invited family and friends over for a celebration. It was a lovely day, filled with activities and performances. I always enjoyed hanging out with Michael, but among my fondest memories of that day was hearing Paula White. I had never heard of her. That evening we all gathered around the outdoor stage to be entertained by singers and dancers.

As a familiar-looking man took the stage, I thought, *Wow, Darryl Strawberry; I didn't know he performed*. I soon learned that the baseball great wasn't there to do that, but to testify about the trials and tribulations he had faced in his career.

Accompanying Strawberry was a smallish, blond woman he introduced as Paula White, his spiritual adviser. When she began to speak and give her testimony, I was in awe. She reminded me of a Baptist preacher from back in the day as she rocked the crowd with her command of God's word. Everyone was moved. Even the crickets seemed to stop chirping to take in White's message.

I was in the middle of my journey to a deeper understanding of my relationship with God, and Pastor White's message of healing, restoration, and encouragement that evening at Neverland was exactly what I needed. When she came off the stage and passed by me, I wanted to shake her hand, but all I could do was stutter, "Wow, totally awesome!"

Several years passed before I rediscovered her through T. D. Jakes' television ministry and conferences. Paula White was high on my list of people I wanted to learn more from about maximizing my 86400. I needed to tap into her wisdom. For White, the relationship between wisdom and purpose management hinges on moving from idea to action.

"If God says, 'Joseph, you are going to have prosperity on earth' while he is deep in a pit, how does this expectation of him being this world changer and history maker line up with his current reality?" she asked. "He has to look at destiny in the overall big picture of things. That's God's way, and when you can arrange the declaration and the decree with the knowledge taken from the word of God, you can put those in proper arrangement. That's when you really begin to see a difference and it is not just wishing and high expectations."

Wishing is not action, Pastor White emphasizes to those

who are lost or confused. "When I meet with people who are struggling, I often pass along these simple steps: One, grieve what you've lost and come to terms with the struggle you're dealing with. Two, face your current reality. Three, align yourself with your desires for the future. Be realistic about where you are, but be adamant that your current reality is not where you're going to stay. Remember: With God, all things are possible.

"Joseph did not remain in the pit and when he was released from it; he was wise enough to seize the opportunities that came his way.

"Typically, we give such diluted portions of ourselves that we become poured out everywhere, and we're not effective anywhere," White said. "The key to avoiding this is using our energy and wisdom effectively within the time frame of a day, and effective application of wisdom brings me into the highest place of quality, quantity, force, and focus.

"We were created to be fruitful and multiply," White told me. "We were created to produce in life. The problem is that there are only 86400 seconds or 24 hours in a day, and when demand to do or produce exceeds capacity, we begin to make poor decisions or expedite choices. So the key is not necessarily our time management but our energy efficiency—the ability to fully engage and manage the energy that every one of us is made of."

White channels her wisdom to move from idea to action each day. "If we are going to maximize our 86400, we must recognize that the number of hours in a day is fixed," she continued. "Our 86400 is fixed, but the quantity and quality of our energy available to us is not. So the more we take responsibility for the quantity and quality of our energy, the more we are empowered to live in that efficiency."

White's words were like a symphony of affirmation for me. As she broke down wisdom as putting ideas into action, I could barely contain my emotions. I was on the right track, living my purpose by helping others move from a state of inertia to active intention and to understand that it is important for us to apply our energy to our purpose to produce results.

For White, the power source for that energy is prayer. "I get up first thing in the morning and talk to the Lord," White says. "It's not some super thing, I just say good morning. Then I get my cup of coffee, read, journal, meditate, and work out."

The recharging routine is the foundation of her 86400, allowing her to harness wisdom and apply it to her purpose daily.

"Afterward, I come back to my computer and prioritize my day," she continued. "I decide what is going to require my focus. Some days I need to replenish and restore. Other days, I bask in the gifts God has given me. Other days, I work nonstop, doing business meetings, or traveling, or speaking. I have to prioritize so there is the balance—an equilibrium that understands and meets my needs spiritually, emotionally, mentally, and physically."

Your Next 600 Seconds

Devote your next 600 seconds to thinking about areas of your life where you need to apply wisdom. Have there been times in your life when you could have benefited from greater wisdom? What would help you grow in wisdom? Think of someone you admire for his or her great wisdom and reflect on the things this role model does that you might adopt to fulfill your purpose.

Seconds for the Spirit

"My son, if you accept my words and store up my commands within you, turning your ear to wisdom and applying your heart to understanding, and if you call out for insight and cry aloud for understanding, and if you look for it as for silver and search for it as for hidden treasure, then you will understand the fear of the Lord and find the knowledge of God. For the Lord gives wisdom, and from his mouth come knowledge and understanding" *(Prov. 2:1–6).*

3

Dedication:
Choosing Your Badwater

*The need for devotion to something outside
ourselves is even more profound than the need for
companionship. If we are not to go to pieces or
wither away, we must have some purpose in life;
for no man can live for himself alone.*
—Ross Parmenter

While mentoring a group of ten college students, I took an unscientific poll: "If you had to name the two people you admire most—your heroes, your role models—who would they be?" To my surprise, eight named professional athletes or TV personalities, one named a teacher and a parent, and one named both parents. It made me sad that the majority of them did not name someone who was accessible to them as their ultimate hero, someone up-close-and-personal from whom they could learn life lessons. There is a gap between lessons learned from persons from afar and lessons learned from persons you can see, touch, and dialogue with.

I feel truly blessed to have my parents as my all-time

heroes. They are a great example of dedication. Their dedication showed me how to live in purpose, making every second of every day count.

My father, Jimmie Red, grew up picking cotton in the fields of Washington, Louisiana. My mother, Hazel Red, grew up in Shreveport, Louisiana, the daughter of farmers. During their first few years of marriage, they picked cotton together. They faced every disadvantage imaginable. Jimmie and Hazel Red enjoyed forty-six years of a loving union in marriage, they shared the experience of raising two well-adjusted children, and later they adopted my younger brother Tyrone. Despite obstacles, they went to college, obtained advanced degrees, had successful careers, and served their community—together. They were dedicated to overcoming and meeting every challenge. I witnessed my parents' dedication on countless occasions and learned from them what it means to live "in your purpose."

Their love for their children was amazing, but it was not expressed via kid-glove parenting. They weren't afraid to employ tough love. (To this day, my mother tells me when I'm right and when I'm wrong. When I call her to complain, she keeps me aware of my purpose.)

When my parents adopted Tyrone, they pretty much adopted his biological mother and his siblings. My mother was dedicated *both* to giving him a better life and keeping him connected to his roots—his biological family. She wanted him to know his family, including us (his adopted family) as well as his biological family. Every major holiday, my mother would bring Tyrone's biological mother and one of his siblings to our home. When his younger brother L'il Willie got in trouble, was arrested, and dropped out of school, my mother took him in and enrolled him in a GED program. I'm proud to say that in May 2010, L'il Willie graduated and received his high-school diploma. Now he is preparing to go into the National Guard knowing he has a loving support system at home. My parents have always been dedicated to giving back whenever and wherever possible.

This same spirit of dedication to service was evident in my parents' careers and community lives. My father was a high-school football, basketball, and track coach, and later he moved on to be a high-school principal. My mother was a teacher and reading specialist. Both went far beyond the call of duty and constantly brought less-fortunate kids home. They instituted needed programs and gave every ounce of their beings to helping develop others. As members of a fraternity (Alpha Phi Alpha) and sorority (Sigma Gamma Rho), both of my parents spent countless hours volunteering, founding community outreach projects, facilitating spelling bees, running scholarship pageants, and serving as church deacons.

Seeing my parents dedicate themselves so freely and totally to their purpose was an example I was able to imitate when seeking my own purpose in life. I realized that my reason for being is not tied to one thing. I have my hands in many pots simultaneously, just as my parents had many spheres of influence. From their example, I was able to divide my purpose into three categories: my purpose as it relates to my career, my family, and my community. Each 86400, then, was an opportunity to live my purpose in these three areas. So, rather than watching the clock and being a slave to calendars, organizers, and to-do lists, a reality and mentality that can be quite draining, I felt freed up to create the reality for my family, my career, and my community service that I always envisioned.

Dedication is self-sacrificing devotion for a purpose. Dedication sets aside minor wants and desires, delays immediate gratification, for the accomplishment of greater things in the future. It replaces activities that provide instantaneous, short-lived pleasure with hard work for a purpose. Purpose cannot exist without dedication.

The past we carry dictates our dedication. Maybe you grew up in a neighborhood where actions that earned immediate gratification were cheered and admired, while deeds whose benefits were cumulative and difficult to quantify, like disciplined studying, were labeled as weak, stupid, or a waste of time. Your past might provide a hurdle to dedication on your journey toward managing your purpose.

Dedication may seem more natural if you were raised in a household where your parents sacrificed to provide better opportunities for their children. It might seem commonplace if your sister or brother earned standout honors in a sport through commitment to practice, or if a relative or mentor gave generously of his or her time to those less fortunate.

Regardless of your past, you have a decision to make regarding your commitment to dedication. The decision you make will directly affect your ability to live your life on purpose. Dedication provides you with a drive to move forward amid challenges and setbacks. Dedication gives you that nudge to get up early because your ultimate goal demands it. Dedication helps you hold your tongue when people try to limit you with their words. Dedication enables you to see possibilities that others don't yet see. Dedication gives you the fire to demand your seat at the table when others try to ignore or belittle your cause. Dedication is critical for a purpose-focused life; it propels you forward against forces that would otherwise hold you back. Dedication took my parents from the cotton fields of Louisiana to worlds that are still expanding because of the many lives they touched.

DEDICATION

My family has a long history of supporting the Southern University (SU) Jaguars (as well as the Louisiana State University [LSU] Tigers) in my home state of Louisiana. I am a huge college football fan and an admirer of Les Miles, head coach of LSU. In five years as head football coach at LSU, Miles has led LSU to a national title, a Southeastern Conference championship, two appearances in the SEC Championship Game, three-straight top-five finishes, and four bowl victories. His success and devotion to family are a winning testament to how dedication can help you be a better manager of your God-given time.

Les Miles
Head coach at Louisiana State University since 2005, former coach at Oklahoma State and former assistant coach at Oklahoma State University, the University of Michigan, the University of Colorado, and the Dallas Cowboys.

Dedication appears to me to be some defined spot. I think that guys who have that, look at their day, their life, the things that are important to them, and it goes beyond their dedication, and it becomes who they are, an identity. Dedication involves a process that you go through to put a good team on the field, the process you go through to be a good husband and father, to have waking thoughts that consume your want for successes in different areas. I think guys that do the job that I do or are really into their careers are dedicated by definition but don't see it that way. They basically enjoy their day. It yanks them out of the bed.

It is trying to prioritize those things that will allow you to be successful, in different areas. The most important piece of the management of my purpose and time to me is to make sure that I am doing the important things—the important things not only in football but also in recruiting and representing LSU, but also as a husband, as a father.

It's when you daydream about those things that you want to get accomplished, when you visualize things that you want to accomplish, it just seems to flow very comfortably in the right direction. I find very little conflict in my day. That's because of my commitment to what I'm doing. I use my time as best I can. I wake my kids up in the morning. When it is possible, I take them to school. Certain times. I work out. My day runs fast, late, and I generally have a smile on my face at the end of the day, and I look forward to the next day.

Some people might call it work, but it's enjoyable. The thing that I have been able to do as best I can is do the important things, to prioritize those things and make those things productive and successful.

My typical day can start a number of ways. It will always have the ability to be flexible to accommodate those things that are important. Now when we are in season, I'm already in the office around 7:30 a.m. Half an hour of recruiting, then we're on a specific piece of the game plan, offense, defense, or special teams. The days change but categorically are very similar—the time we get started, time we practice, time our guys go to school, time they study. There is a piece where you can't be too rigid, because creativity is a part of this, and you must allow for flexibility for those people who will be and can be creative in your world or your product.

There is also flexibility in parenting, flexibility in understanding, in change and in how you have to approach situations and problems. The job I have in many instances is a problem-solving job. Identifying the problem and identifying the answer is certainly a part of my day. You plan it and leave room for creativity and flexibility.

It is an absolute must to be conscious of your 86400. If you are not, days are being yanked away from you, and you are not doing the things that you need to be doing. When you are conscious of your 86400, you understand the importance of prioritizing the important things. You must continue to be conscious of what is going on with your time, because if you don't, your time will lapse, and you will not get things done.

I pride myself on my ability to focus. In order to pursue excellence, to be the very best and to do it on many levels, you must be focused. The only way to accomplish that is to focus on where you are going and what you are doing.

When motivating and leading a team, it comes down to a number of things, from organizing a practice schedule, looking at a recruiting map, being able to display honestly a great opportunity for a young quarterback at LSU. No matter what it is that you are doing, you have to want to be the very best. To focus on that desire is what drives you. It also will allow you to manage your time effectively and appropriately.

Once you settle on those things that make you happy, don't let anyone tell you "No!" Just go hard at it, relentlessly, with great effort, enthusiasm, and dedication.

Badwater

When someone first told me about Badwater, I laughed because things like the Badwater Ultramarathon don't happen in real life, only in Clint Eastwood and Bruce Willis movies where macho men disarm bombs with their eyelashes and save the world while suffering 20,000 gunshot wounds to the chest, but in real life? No, certainly not.

Yet Badwater happens in July of every year, and it has since 1987. Over ninety of the world's most Lance Armstrong–esque men and women gather in Death Valley, California, to participate in a 135-mile run to Mount Whitney, California, running in temperatures of up to 130 degrees Fahrenheit. This has to be one of the most extreme and grueling sports anywhere.

After my friend told me about Badwater and I realized it wasn't a hilarious joke, my question was: People actually do this? People feel compelled to run 135 miles through a place called Death Valley? I don't want to drive through that place, much less force my own two feet to carry me across ground so hot it could sizzle fajitas.

Yes, people do this and love it. Many are driven to compete in this event, and the word you could use to describe them, aside from crazy, is dedicated.

Arthur Webb competed in—and finished—the Badwater Ultramarathon nine times, and wrote "Badwater and Extreme Event Survival Tips," on the Web site www.badwater.com's training page.

To prepare for Badwater, Arthur said he ran 120 miles per week for three months, made daily gym visits where he cross-trained on bikes, and did an absurd number of sit-ups.

After each of his workouts, he spent an hour in a 170-degree sauna. The heat training was necessary to prepare for the desert heat that would blast at his skin and cook his interior while he was in Death Valley.

Arthur elaborated on preparation for every facet of the race: skin protection, cooling, feet apparel, blisters, rest stops, pacers, electrolytes, nutrition, and hydration. He used a slew of running terms that flew right over my head. His last piece of advice was most crucial: "Please, no groveling or whining," he said. "Your responsibility is to stand tall and silently deal with the pain, misery, and suffering and to finish the race. Don't forget, you were the one who filled out the race application."

I still wonder why people would endure that incredibly grueling training and face such hardship just to say they finished a race. I won't suggest that anyone sign up for Badwater, but I can see an incredibly valuable lesson in all that sweat and running in Death Valley. It's called dedication—profound devotion and attachment to a specific purpose or goal.

We live in a culture that speaks fluent immediate satisfaction. We want a hamburger; we go to McDonald's. We want coffee; we go to Starbucks. We have On Demand TV, downloadable eBooks, and breaking news via text message. Nearly everything is produced instantaneously so no one will have to experience the terror of "waiting." We get what we want, when we want. 1 Corinthians 9:24–27 says, "Do you not know that in a race all the runners run, but only one gets the prize? Run in such a way as to get the prize. Everyone who competes in the games goes into strict training. They do it to get a crown that will not last; but we do it to get a crown that will last forever. Therefore I do not run like a man running aimlessly; I do not fight like a man beating the air. No, I beat my body and make it my slave so that after I have preached to others, I myself will not be disqualified for the prize."

God has called us to lives of excellence and investment, given us each 86400 so that we might engage, contribute, and truly make an indelible mark in our world. Pleasing God involves dedication, and dedication requires endurance, hardship, patience.

I have a friend who grew up in the church. She went to Sunday school every weekend, singing "Jesus Loves Me" while spilling red Kool-Aid on her home-stitched dress. She learned all about Noah and the Ark, the wise men, and the Crucifixion. Now, when Sundays roll around, she spends her day running errands, folding laundry, or glued to the couch catching up on Turner Classic Movies. When I ask her about her faith, she says she still believes in God; she just likes sleeping in. She likes to be selfish with her lazy Sundays.

Many of us choose selfish pleasure over true dedication. We are "too busy" to have our daily devotionals. We find time to pray only when problems arise. We watch news about the poor and widows on TV and confine our response to words of sympathy that stay in our living rooms, rather than act with kindness and generosity toward those in need. Garrison Keillor is widely credited for this quote: "Anyone who thinks sitting in church can make you a Christian must also think that sitting in a garage can make you a car."

Second Thessalonians 3:11–13 reads, "We hear that some among you are idle. They are not busy; they are busybodies. Such people we command and urge in the Lord Jesus Christ to settle down and earn the bread they eat. And as for you, brothers, never tire of doing what is right."

God continually challenges us to be individuals who choose dedication over idleness and action over complacency. We must set aside our selfish and lazy ways and never tire of doing what is right and what is good. We must approach our relationships, an opportunity, or a life goal with dedication. We are to invest ourselves, be willing to do the hard things. The outcome will be enhanced a million-fold. God never promised us that things would be easy. He just promised us that He would be with us, continually, as we experience them, and that He will be our well of strength from which we can continually draw encouragement, energy, and faith. He will be with us through our Badwaters.

Temptations

Dedication, or setting aside immediate gratification for a future goal, is critical for living life on purpose. Dedication also means confronting and defeating temptations.

I consider myself a creative person with a slight case of ADD when it comes to my career. I was not always living on purpose, particularly in my career. I know that being an educator is my calling. Teaching, mentoring, and sharing knowledge is my reason for being. I enjoy speaking to groups of kids and writing children's books with moral lessons, as well as books for adults. I get excited about being a teacher and educator. It is what gets me up in the morning. Yet it is also what I fought against doing for many years.

I earned a bachelor's degree in mathematics and a master's degree in education, came to Houston, taught for a short time, and became an instructional supervisor for mathematics in the Houston Independent School District. I was happy, but I allowed temptations to draw me away from my true purpose. I had a hard time dedicating myself to education and sticking to it.

In the early 1990s, I met teen rappers 2Low and Awol from the group the Blac Monks. I began managing them and I started a record label. I liked designing T-shirts, so I created a line of T-shirts called American-Statements. I opened a sports marketing company with my best friend, WNBA Hall of Famer Cynthia Cooper. I had opportunities that I would not turn down. Remarkably, most of my ventures were successful. I was making money. However, the more money I made, the farther away I moved from my purpose. I was not happy.

I continued along this path, jumping from venture to venture. I was a stockbroker, real-estate agent, and marketing executive. I woke up one morning and decided I wanted to be in the oil business. I looked on the map, picked Angola, and, with Cynthia, I went there looking for oil deals, gold, and diamonds—during their civil war! The country was on the State Department's "do not travel" list, but I went anyway. God is good all the time, because, miraculously, no harm came to us.

While in Angola, we encountered difficulties, but success found me again in a much different form. I went to Africa looking for oil, gold, and diamonds—but found a divine calling. God put a plan in action that touched my heart. I found myself engaged in activities that were not on my to-do list: visiting schools and hospitals. The people I met during those unplanned excursions changed me in a profound way. I arrived in Angola to see what I could take away and left with a dedication to give. Back in Houston, I became one of the founding members and first president of the Houston-

Luanda Sister City Association. Our organization was dedicated to serving others, and soon my divine purpose—as teacher and educator—once again came to the fore.

Still, I just put my foot into the education pool. I didn't dive all the way in. I served as special adviser and consultant to U.S. Secretary of Education Rod Paige, taught classes at Prairie View A&M University, and wrote more books. Over time, I noticed that I felt joy and fulfillment when I was involved in education. Conversely, the business deals brought me money but not joy. I began to dedicate myself to doing what God put in my heart. I learned to say no to temptations.

Believe me, they still come. Yet now I'm able to ask these questions before I jump: Does this feed into my purpose? Is this what I'm dedicated to?

Education does not just take place in a classroom. I'm engaged on a number of fronts. Every Child an Author, a company I co-founded with my friends Vuthy Kuon and Charles Nguyen, helps K–12 students become published authors. I'm an education contributor for the *Dialogue with Ada* radio show, through which I share my academic expertise on curriculum and other education issues, I head up the *86400 Book Club for Kids*, which airs monthly on Fox 26 in Houston, and my educational consultant company is in partnership to create a leadership institute at a college in Houston. This institute will engage in training, seminars, research, and conferences centered around the development of servant leadership skills and civic engagement. My involvement is immersive.

Temptations come in various ways but have a common effect—distracting you from managing your purpose. Temptations compete for your time and attention, and when they win, you find yourself wrestling with questions of meaning and substance, asking yourself, Where did all the time go?

Idleness is a threat to our dedication, but it's not the root of the problem. It is the symptom of something much bigger: temptation. Whenever we make a decision in our lives, we are choosing one thing over another. We choose to live as a hope-filled victor rather than as a helpless victim. We choose to go on a diet to take care of rising blood pressure rather than indulge in stroke-inviting foods. We choose to budget for the coming year instead of living by the seat of our pants. When we make these choices, we are choosing to give certain things up: defeatist attitudes and actions, our love of fast food, our desire for a new car. We are living lives of dedication—setting aside short-term thrills for long-term joys.

Making the decision can be easy; following through with it is much harder. How many New Year's resolutions have you made to go to the gym three times a week or maybe give up caffeine? While the goal is good, how hard is it to stick with it when the alarm goes off at 6:00 a.m. and another hour of sleep seems far more appealing than walking on a treadmill? Or when you start to feel that midafternoon grogginess coming on and begin craving that espresso pick-me-up?

Dedication requires overcoming internal opposition—fighting off temptation that lingers and lures you back into your old ways. We have to remain cognizant of our purpose, mindful of the end goal, and faithful in our pursuit of it.

Consider Jesus' temptations. At the beginning of His ministry, He was led by the Spirit into the desert, where He was tempted for forty days (Luke 4:1–13). The devil offered Him food to nourish His hunger, the promise of power over all kingdoms of the world, and the challenge to test God's protection. Jesus remained devoted to God, faithful to the

Scriptures. His dedication and understanding gave Him strength, and the devil didn't win. We will constantly be lured by temptation. We will frequently be given the opportunities to satisfy our personal, unhealthy desires, and it is up to us to be dedicated to our purpose, to choose the hard road that leads to the highest payoff.

The Need to be Rooted

Dedication is essential if you want to make the most of your God-given time, but is dedication always a positive? Is there a flip side? Dedication implies passion, ferocity, faithfulness. While that can be an asset as we navigate through life's temptations, dedication can grow to be a temptation itself, and lead us away from what is healthy, what is best for us. With extreme submission to an idea or a cause, dedication can become ungodly and put our heart in harm's way.

In *Outliers* (Little, Brown and Company, 2008), Malcolm Gladwell, who repeatedly produces best-selling books, talks about how greatness, whether in sports, music, or intellectual pursuits, requires a specific and focused commitment—hours and hours of practice, study, research, and trial and error that most people don't view as sensible. Dedication can imply a nearly irrational commitment; there is only a hairline difference between dedication and detrimental pursuit. How does one find that line? How can one be sure not to step over it? The Bible gives us direction on this. Matthew 6:22 reads, "No one can serve two masters. Either he will hate the one and love the other, or he will be devoted to the one and despise the other."

God cautions us about our temptation to invest ourselves

in unhealthy ways. He knows that dedication can become twisted and distance us from God's will rather than bring us closer to Him. God instilled desires within us. He gave us talents and ambitions. He embedded desires in our hearts so that we might seek to make His goodness come to fruition on this earth. The verse in Matthew isn't telling us that we should ignore our heart's desires and our dreams. It's telling us to integrate our relationship with God into our pursuits. Christ should be the center of all things. He should be the binding cord in our marriage, the essential link in our friendships, the sturdy roots in our profession, and the driving force behind our greatest imaginings.

Proverbs 3:5–6 reads, "Trust in the LORD with all your heart and lean not on your own understanding; in all your ways acknowledge him and he will make your paths straight." What an incredible promise. If we acknowledge Christ in all areas of our life, He will be the integral force and support system behind what we pursue. Because of Him, we can pour out all our love with strength and courage, and know that is intertwined intimately with His will. Because of Him, things like Badwater aren't impossible after all.

86400 Adviser: Ralph de la Vega—Dedication

Ralph de la Vega's first lesson in dedication came after he arrived in the United States as a ten-year-old from Cuba, alone because his parents and sister had to stay behind.

It was 1962 and his family had tried to board a plane together en route to Miami, Florida, to flee the communist regime of Fidel Castro. A Cuban official claimed that the papers for the rest of the family were not in order. Only he had clearance to go. On the spot, Ralph's parents made the heart-wrenching and brave decision to allow him his freedom. Hasty arrangements were made by telephone for him to stay with a friend of an aunt for what was to be a few days before his parents and young sister could join him.

"I was expecting that they would arrive shortly after me, but days and weeks passed and they didn't come," he recalled. "But rather than focus on all the negative aspects of the situation that I was in—a new country, a new language, et cetera—I dedicated myself to looking at the positive side of things. I was in the greatest country in the world, the land of opportunity. Even though my parents weren't with me yet and wouldn't be for some time, I focused on the blessings. That kept me going through what was probably the most difficult stage in my life."

This dedication to optimism had to keep him going for four years until he was reunited with his parents, and that way of thinking stayed with him. "It is that same spirit of no matter how tough a situation is that I face, I look for the positive," he said. "I look for the opportunities and I dedicate myself to making the most of them."

A friend of mine who had read de la Vega's book, *Obstacles Welcome: Turn Adversity into Advantage in Business and Life*, written with Paul B. Brown (Thomas Nelson, 2009), had talked often to me about this moving story of an immigrant child rising to such an influential position. As I looked for role models to consult for this book, de la Vega was one of the individuals I had to pursue. Fortunately, my very good friend David Dunham, a former publishing executive, was kind enough to introduce me to him.

De la Vega is AT&T's president and CEO of Mobility and Consumer Markets. He had worked his way up from

being a managing assistant to lead all consumer marketing, sales, content, converged services, and customer care
for the company's wireless and wired businesses. I was also
impressed with how the iPhone he helped bring to market
had increased my productivity and made my use of new
technology less intimidating. Surely this must be a person
who had something to say about dedication.

"I've never found something in my life or in business that
ever came easy," he told me. "They all require quite a bit of
dedication, and being dedicated and knowing what you are
dedicated to helps you make the best use of your time."

Dedication kept him focused as he pursued his education,
often cleaning bathrooms or sweeping floors to earn money,
as he describes in his book. He holds a bachelor's degree
of science in mechanical engineering from Florida Atlantic
University, and an MBA from Northern Illinois University,
but he said he regards his education merely as a foundation,
a key asset but one that he has to renew continually.

"I realized the minute I stepped out of the university that
I would become obsolete if I didn't keep up with what was
happening in the world," he told me. "Getting a good education and staying up to date has probably been the most
beneficial tool in my success. That's why my message to
young people is exactly that. I tell them to stay in school and
get the best education you can, because that opens doors.
Without any question I would not be sitting here talking to
you had I not had a good education and kept current with
the things that are happening. Education is that tool."

Dedication has allowed de la Vega to live his purpose as
an institutional change agent. "One of the most difficult
things I had to get done in the business world was complete
a merger of two very large operations, AT&T Wireless and

Cingular," said de la Vega. "Completing a merger in business is what I would almost call the Super Bowl of business. It is a very tough thing to do."

To recruit people who could help him succeed, he said, "I interviewed individuals for this task before we put them on the team. I wanted to make sure that they had the capability and the commitment to dedicate two years of their career, of their time, day in and day out—86400 in and 86400 out—to do this. We were successful because of that team's dedication of time and their commitment.

"Most mergers are not successful, because companies end up getting less than what they thought they were going to get," he explained.

De la Vega recalls that he also had to apply that same level of commitment to make the iPhone a reality.

"It took a lot of dedication—of effort—to work with a company like Apple that had never made a phone and was trying to implement something that was going to drastically change an industry," he recalled. "That also took a very dedicated team, working for many months trying to make the contract and the project a reality for us. But all of this kind of ties together in that I think that all of these tough things to do, whether they are of a personal nature or of a business nature—commitment, dedication, discipline, sacrifice—they all kind of go together."

During Ralph de la Vega's thirty-six-plus years in the telecommunications industry, he has also worked for Cingular and Bell South, where he served as president of the Latin American division with responsibility for operations in eleven countries.

As a person with a full plate, de la Vega sees dedication as a way to maximize efficiency—getting the biggest purpose bang for the buck. He is chairman of a leading wireless industry trade group, is involved in numerous nonprofit and community organizations, including Junior Achievement Worldwide and the Boy Scouts of America, and is also a husband and father. "Dedication helps me be a better manager of my time and purpose because it helps me to focus," he said. "Once you have a large number of things that you've got going on, a key factor in doing them all and doing them well is being focused on the things that really matter. You have to be very disciplined and dedicated to doing those things that really matter and not worrying too much about the things that don't."

For de la Vega, focusing on your purpose is key to being effective each day. "If you are not conscious of your 86400, you are not going to be able to balance priorities well. Nobody has found a way yet to manufacture time. That's the one thing that once it is gone, you can't get it back. So making sure that you adhere to a disciplined schedule and that the people you interact with are respectful of that schedule is the key," said de la Vega.

Sticking to a schedule requires planning, which puts dedication and discipline into practice. "In my life, I don't wait to plan," de la Vega said. "Often, I book things a year in advance, getting the crucial things scheduled in, so I can approach them intentionally and prepared." To him, dedication is a purpose-management tool.

"Dedication absolutely begins my day," he explained. "I've made it a point to try to lead a healthy lifestyle so that I am able to do and accomplish the things that I need to throughout the course of my day—my 86400, if you will. I'm pretty busy, I travel all over the place, but I always try to get up and exercise—something that isn't easy when you've been on the road or have worked a long day the day before. The discipline to do it is essential and that takes dedication."

Exercising daily is "a very small example," he added, "but I think in order for people to make the best of themselves, of their 86400, they have to be disciplined. It's essential for the most tactical, as well as visionary, things that a person does in their life."

He starts early on his 86400 and leaves little to chance as the day progresses. "My iPhone alarm wakes me up around 4:30 a.m. I then turn my iPod on and do my workout routine," he continued. "Because the planning is already done, I know what I have to accomplish or follow back up on. I think getting a good start to the day, feeling good about yourself from a physical point of view, is the key to having a good day. Because obstacles will come up so you may as well start with a good positive attitude, and hopefully you will end your day with one as well, a good attitude."

For those struggling with purpose and productivity, de la Vega suggested, "The first thing you should do is examine your purpose and find your passion. Getting yourself centered as to what your purpose is or what you are passionate about is key."

He said he would also tell those who feel lost "to dream big—dream really, really big—about what you could be and never let anyone put limitations on what you can accomplish. You'll run across obstacles that often seem overwhelming, but they're easily overcome when you feel a sense of purpose and passion about what you do."

Obviously, de la Vega has been no stranger to obstacles, but what helped him survive unfathomable challenges as a child immigrant—his commitment to dedication—empowers him today to remain a successful CEO of one of the largest global companies. The executive's strict dedication to his purpose and his ability to maintain a laser-like focus on his purpose-filled goals frames his 86400s for maximum efficiency and allows him to be a positive force in the global world of business and the wider community.

Your Next 600 Seconds

It's evident that God has called us to a life of dedication rather than a life of idleness. It's true, too, that He wants that dedication to be intimately and continually linked with Him. Devote your next 600 seconds to understanding how dedication can help you make the most of your God-given time. Consider whether you are truly dedicated to your purposes. For de la Vega, one of the most effective practices he does is plan. How can you more efficiently manage your purpose through planning?

Apply the principle to your own life. Have you been able to stay dedicated to a cause or goal even amid doubts, setbacks, and disappointments? If so, how? If not, why?

Seconds for the Spirit

> *"Enter through the narrow gate. For wide is the gate and broad is the road that leads to destruction, and many enter through it. But small is the gate and narrow the road that leads to life, and only a few find it"* (Matt. 7:13–14).

THE PRESENT WE LIVE

──────

The present is truly God's gift to us because in it all that we can ever do takes place. Whatever we accomplish will be the result of actions taken in the present—the here and now. The past affects what we do or don't do in the present. The future inspires us to take action right now. But living your purpose boils down to what you are willing to do today. This makes the present the most critical time regarding purpose.

Years ago, Janet Jackson asked a pertinent question with her song "What Have You Done for Me Lately?" She implied that our past actions are dead and gone, and if we want to have an impact today, we have to get busy in the present. The late John Lennon waxed poetic about the potential of the future in his classic song "Imagine." Yet potential dies on the vine without efforts to maximize it in the present. If you want to master your purpose, the present is what matters.

Many of us grew up reading *The Velveteen Rabbit* when we were children. The book, first published in 1922, tells the story of a stuffed toy rabbit that was given as a Christmas present to a young boy. While there are other fancier toys for the boy to play with, he clings to the rabbit as his best friend. Even as the years drag on and the rabbit loses its shine and newness, the boy still loves it deeply.

> *"What is REAL?" asked the Rabbit one day, when they were lying side by side near the nursery fender, before Nana came to tidy the room. "Does it mean having things that buzz inside you and a stick-out handle?"*
>
> *"Real isn't how you are made," said the Skin Horse. "It's a thing that happens to you. When a child loves you for a long, long time, not just to play with, but REALLY loves you, then you become Real."*
>
> *"Does it hurt?" asked the Rabbit.*
>
> *"Sometimes," said the Skin Horse, for he was always truthful. "When you are Real you don't mind being hurt."*
>
> *"Does it happen all at once, like being wound up," he asked, "or bit by bit?"*
>
> *"It doesn't happen all at once," said the Skin Horse. "You become. It takes a long time. That's why it doesn't happen often to people who break easily, or have sharp edges, or who have to be carefully kept. Generally, by the time you are Real, most of your hair has been loved off, and your eyes drop out and you get loose in the joints and very shabby. But these things don't matter at all, because once you are Real you can't be ugly, except to people who don't understand."*
>
> —Margery Williams,
> *The Velveteen Rabbit* (Avon, 1922)

At its core, even though it's a children's story, *The Velveteen Rabbit* speaks to the heart of being human. It's a story about discovering what is real, discovering one's significance. We all seek to understand our identity. It is not found in our past or in the future, but only in one's present.

Henry Ford, according to www.thinkexist.com, once said, "The only history that's worth a tinker's damn is the history we make today." I can't disregard the past as easily as Ford, but I understand his point. Similarly, Sir Winston Churchill, also according to www.thinkexist.com, warned those fixated upon the future, "It is a mistake to look too far ahead. The chain of destiny can only be grasped one link at a time." To make the most of any given day or moment, you must be able to live in the present. Wisdom calls us to be present in our present.

Living in the present is not as simple as it sounds. It is a talent, an acquired skill, for we are constantly tempted to focus our gaze upon days past or moments not yet here. Everything from our movies to our music, our novels to our newscasts, seeks to draw our attention away from the "right now" and place it on some yesterday or tomorrow.

The present is where the action is. The present is where yesterday's hopes and hard lessons converge with our big dreams of tomorrow. The present we live is the only tangible reality we know at any given moment. In the present, we can maximize our purpose output each day in both positive and negative ways. The present can provide peace, happiness, and a well-earned release from past hurts or future worries. It can also be so comfortable that each "right now" moment is another moment wasted.

Three principles must be incorporated into your daily practices to live a purposeful present: balance, imagination, and thankfulness. Together they help you move effectively from thought to action, master the art of making the most of every day, hour, minute, and second, and live your purpose.

4

Balance:
An Act of Love

Happiness is not a matter of intensity but
of balance, order, rhythm and harmony.
—Thomas Merton

Not too long ago, I struggled because I woke in the mornings feeling either ecstatic or exasperated. I knew something was wrong. I was doing and experiencing so much, because I had so many opportunities, but I was not giving them my best. I was spreading myself so thin that I couldn't fully immerse myself in any one undertaking.

None of the time-management strategies I learned over the years helped me. I was so overwhelmed that I was paralyzed, unable to do anything. I dropped all projects and disappointed a lot of people. Yet that radical act is part of what saved me. My approach was extreme, and I'm not suggesting you do what I did. I had to pare down and clear my schedule so I could enjoy some downtime. Taking that time off, resting and just doing nothing, reminded me of a poem I wrote when I was in the sixth grade. I was frustrated with the Vinyettes, a dance group I had started. We had three events coming up. We weren't prepared because we were all busy doing too many other things.

I asked my mom if she remembered that poem I wrote so many years ago. Not only did she remember it, she had a copy of it. She was concerned that even as a child I was prone to take on too much.

Stop the Merry-Go-Round

Stop the Merry-Go-Round, I got to get off
I got to get away and meditate in my Hay Loft
Who am I, do I even want to know
If I can't do it, who will complete the show
Too much to do and no time to do it right
Make a clone of me before we lose the fight

Okay, I won't be called to recite a poem at the next presidential inauguration, but it amazes me how juggling, taking on too much, can start at a very young age.

We need time to evaluate, review, and set priorities that line up with our purpose. That abrupt stop cleared my head and allowed me to ask, Why am I here and what am I doing with my gift of 86400? That break helped me to quit trying to manage time, a concept with limits, and focused me on the management of my purpose, a concept that is limitless.

Thus, time management is an act dedicated to juggling and sorting a limited entity. It's like trying to expand your culinary horizons to taste all that life has to offer, yet all you have at your disposal is chicken. Sure, chicken can be prepared in a multitude of ways, but at the end of the day, you are still limited. Chicken will never be salmon, rib eye, or anything other than what it is. At the end of the day, though you can get quite creative in your preparation, whatever you prepare is going to taste like chicken. How limiting.

Seeing life through the lens of a daily gift of 86400 seconds led me to recognize that the real power, purpose, and productivity I was looking for could be achieved only by managing my purpose, rather than by managing my time.

Purpose management is a concept that allows you unlimited possibilities. Moving things around on your things-to-do list, such as switching when you will go shopping for groceries from 11 a.m. to 6 p.m. may allow you more time on a certain task. Such a move can be quite helpful. But the danger in just managing time comes from moving around tasks yet never truly evaluating how those tasks reflect your higher calling, your divine purpose, your reason for being.

Slowly, over the course of a year, I began to identify the elements that I needed in my life to help me manage my purpose. I turned to my instruction manual, the Bible. It shaped my thoughts on the ten characteristics I'm sharing with you in this book.

Real versus Make-Believe

In the movie *The Karate Kid*, a 2010 remake of the 1984 classic, the master teacher, Mr. Han (Jackie Chan), provides his pupil Dre Parker (Jaden Smith) with a lesson on the importance of balance. In the middle of their grueling training schedule for an upcoming martial arts tournament, Mr. Han takes Dre on a seemingly unrelated excursion into the Chinese countryside. The break from the rigors of practice helps Dre understand the spiritual principles behind the martial art. Without giving away too much of the movie, during the field trip Dre picks up knowledge that proves crucial during his final tournament battle. Had it not been for that break and others throughout his training period, Dre may never have maximized his Karate Kid potential. Giving yourself ample time to work, play, rest, and rejuvenate provides balance crucial to living a life of purpose and maximizing your 86400.

Botanist, educator, and inventor George Washington Carver is best known for discovering and developing hundreds of products and uses for the peanut. What many people don't know is that Carver received the insights that led to his discoveries during his early morning walks in the woods. His meditative strolls opened him to "hear" the plants share their secrets with him. Carver would then casually walk back to his lab and put into action the knowledge and wisdom he received while enjoying what seemed to be downtime. When purpose becomes a part of who you are, you have no downtime. Your time relaxing, resting, and rejuvenating becomes just as important and productive to your outcomes as time spent doing work-related tasks. This is the power of the principle of balance. Balance feeds your whole self—mind, body, and spirit. It allows purpose to infuse every part of your being.

BALANCE

*For me, part of having a balanced life is to have a balanced
diet, and among those who know me well, it's no secret that one
of my favorite chain restaurants to get a healthy bite is Subway.
I was elated when Les Winograd at Subway informed me that
one of their executives, Don Fertman, would speak to me about
how being balanced helps him be a better manager of his time
and purpose.*

Don Fertman
Director of development for Doctor's Associates, Inc., parent company of Subway, since 1998, and a former freelance writer,
musician, and jingle writer for the company.

Balance is one of those things I've spent billions of seconds trying
to achieve. Balance was a real challenge to me. When I was
in my early thirties, I came up with the idea of putting the components of my life into buckets. There was the work bucket that
was always full and overflowing, taking up most of my 86400
seconds, the family bucket—in my early thirties, I was single so
that didn't require a lot of attention—and then the social bucket.
In my thirties I wanted that one overflowing. So I thought, Gee, if
I could get all these buckets filled with the right proportion of time
and the attention they require, I would be on the right path.

So my concept of balance is filling all my buckets proportion-
ately. Maybe one bucket requires 30 percent of my time and
another bucket 60 percent of my time, et cetera. You have to
prioritize those buckets. The work one is the one that pays the
bills. The work one is very rewarding to me. I have the good
fortune of working for a company (Subway) that is growing very

quickly and that has a lot of new things going on, for instance, introducing breakfast. I'm involved in a very dynamic business, a very dynamic industry. So devoting time to that particular bucket is always attractive to me. . . . Now, in my fifties, I've got a family. I have two relatively young children. I've got friends. I have a different kind of life now. So my buckets are the same, but the time I devote to each one of them changes over time.

One of the things I discovered back when I was figuring out my bucket theory was that there was a spiritual bucket and that particular bucket for me was quite empty. Some of the things I was hearing drew me to that spiritual bucket. I thought that if I devoted some time to filling the spiritual bucket, I would more naturally achieve a balance in the process. So I devoted some of my seconds to that new direction, and, somewhere along the line, I discovered that it worked. I became more comfortable in my life. I was more centered and more balanced, at least for the moment. It is all moment by moment, and life can get off balance at any given moment. You have to prioritize and know when to shift what percentage of time to what bucket.

I have a spiritual program that I follow. It ultimately guides me in everything I do. I've been with Subway for twenty-nine years, and they have given me all kinds of opportunities. I've had a chance to grow with the business. It's been very rewarding and fulfilling. A lot of the success I've had here at Subway is due to me having the right perspective, and I get that from my spiritual bucket. My spiritual program is kind of a twelve-step program, as we call them, and it's got to do with making sure that I'm right with the people in my life—that I do the right thing. At any given point in my 86400 when I have a difficult choice to make, I try to do the right thing. If I have a situation that is puzzling or baffling, I make sure I get advice about it.

My spiritual program is loosely Bible-based. It is not adherent to any particular religion, and it takes into account various philosophies.

My first moment of the day, I take time out to thank what I call my higher power for waking me up. Now I have another day, another 86400, ahead of me. I usually head for the shower. I go wake the kids up. I tell them I love them. I wish them a good day. I tell my wife that as well. I listen to positive motivational-type things on my way to work, while in the car. I get to my desk and go about my day. Any given day could be any combination of things: calls, meetings, presentations, sometimes getting on a plane going somewhere. Every day is a little bit different, so I look forward to each and every 86400 seconds.

Every second of my day is something different, so as a result I need to be conscious of where I'm spending my time, what I'm spending my time on, who I'm spending my time with. I need to be less conscious of what I have done, my accomplishments of the last seconds, hours, or years. I strive to be much more conscious of this moment, this second, of who I am this second, because I never know if I'm going to have the next second, the next 86400.

There is a lot of credence given to multitasking, and that's great. That works in situations when I need to pay general attention to things, but when full concentration is required, when I really need to concentrate in order to do a terrific job, it is better that I put all my attention on that one thing—until something else distracts me, of course.

My day works for me because I'm *on purpose*. I go about my day managing my purpose within the time that I have. I look at the time I have and the job I have to do. Then I try to make every second count in a positive way. I think this purpose management concept you are bringing forth is a really great way to look at it. If I was to give someone advice or encouragement, it's simply just "Take some time to find out who you are." It is not who you are in your job title. It is not who you are in your family responsibilities—the labels—but who you really are. What makes you get up in the morning? What stirs the passion inside of you? What makes your heart beat? What makes you feel good at the end of the day and causes you to say, "This was really a great day"?

There was a movie with Dustin Hoffman, and in this movie, *Little Big Man* (1970), he was adopted by a Native American tribe. The chief would say now and then, "Today is a good day to die." I've actually had that feeling. Not that I've wanted to die, but if I died that day, it would be okay, because I did everything I wanted to do that day. I feel good about the day. I feel good about myself. I've lived my life to its fullest. I feel that all is truly well. I can understand that concept. I've done it all, and today is a good day to die. So find out what makes you tick, what makes you happy, who you are. Not husband, director of development, not Dad. What wakes you up in the morning?

Changing a Diaper and Butchering a Hog

When I begin the day my eyelids stutter open, and the first thought of that particular 86400 enters my mind. When I've had a good night's rest, my mind is bouncing. I'm excited about getting out of bed and getting started on what can only be prosperous and fulfilling new adventures. If I've slept poorly, eaten unhealthily, if I have loads on my agenda, and an overdue to-do list, I wake up with a strained heart. I automatically know what I'm up against and so the bounce becomes a crawl.

Many of us wake up with the weight of extensive obligations. We have become "multitaskers" and "well-rounded" individuals whose typical day is typically overwhelming. Our goal-setting, shoot-for-the-stars mentality has transformed our 86400s from healthy and productive to impossible and fruitless.

The science fiction writer Robert Heinlein once wrote, "A human being should be able to change a diaper, plan an invasion, butcher a hog, conn a ship, design a building, write a sonnet, balance accounts, build a wall, set a bone, comfort the dying, take orders, give orders, cooperate, act alone, solve equations, analyze a new problem, pitch manure, program a computer, cook a tasty meal, fight efficiently, die gallantly."

Merely reading that quote exhausts me. There is so much going on: ships, pigs, bones. Yet Heinlein's quote isn't that far from the truth. In our daily lives, we have so much to get done. We have work and school. We have family and friends. We have dinner parties and doctor's appointments. We have errands to run, mouths to feed, pews to fill, events to attend, people to call, laundry to wash, beds to make, cars to drive, grass to mow, books to read—and, well, the list goes on and on and on. The blessing and curse of the progress in the twenty-first century is the flexibility it's given us. Opportunities abound. We can get to places more quickly and do things faster, so we try to squeeze in more and more. As a result, we've become overcommitters. We've plunged into opportunities headfirst without thinking about how we're going to accomplish it all—and, more importantly, how we're going to accomplish it *well*.

God calls us to "be still" and trust in His plans. He does not call us to run around aimlessly from commitment to commitment. " 'For I know the plans I have for you,' declares the LORD, 'plans to prosper you and not to harm you, plans to give you hope and a future' " (Jer. 29:11).

As I thought and prayed about balance, I began to ask myself what were the weights in my bag. Was I carrying around too many? Were these all God-given? Proverbs 16:11 says, "Honest scales and balances are from the LORD; all the weights in the bag are of his making." Was I distributing them well, living a life of equilibrium, a life of purpose?

A mature individual who lives a healthy, purpose-filled 86400 is, at the core, balanced. Balance is the mental steadiness and emotional stability that generates calm, intentional behavior and judgment. Those who are balanced create a grounded center in their lives. They understand how to pursue life's opportunities with poise, peace, and purpose.

Colossians 1:16–17 reads, "For by him all things were created: things in heaven and on earth, visible and invisible, whether thrones or powers or rulers or authorities; all things were created by him and for him. He is before all things, and in him all things hold together."

God is explicit in His hopes for our life. God is the great equilibrium. He is the tie that binds all the disconnected aspects of our life—our professions, our families, our friends, our dreams—and He is the root that infuses health and prosperity into our pursuits—"in him, all things hold together" (Col. 1:17).

Another Scripture, I Corinthians 12:14–15, 18, has always painted a vivid picture of balance to me, depicting the body's parts as essential components of the greater whole: "Now the body is not made up of one part but of many. If the foot should say, 'Because I am not a hand, I do not belong to the body,' it would not for that reason cease to be a part of the body. . . . But in fact God has arranged the parts in the body, every one of them, just as he wanted them to be".

The various aspects of your life must work together; they are all significant parts. They must all be on the same page, working toward a common purpose.

We are connected individuals and not separate entities, each working for our own personal benefit.

How can we attain balance? Give up the lion's share of self-control, and fix God at the center of our lives.

The Lion's Share

Many people believe that all of life is a quest for balance—a state of harmony and inner peace that can allow you to weather life's storms as well as enjoy its victories. Ancient spiritualists, as well as New Age religionists, refer to this quest as the human need for mind, body, and spirit integration, which is often referred to as holistic health. In Chinese philosophy, this quest is symbolized by the concept of yin-yang, the existence of complementary opposites or opposing forces within the greater whole. Yin-yang constantly inter-acts, never existing in absolute stasis. This is an important point because it reminds us that our quest for balance is never-ending. We are always moving closer to or away from this desired state of equilibrium, and thus we must always be mindful, moment by moment, of how our actions affect our journey.

Finding such harmony isn't easy. The challenge we face in this life-consuming quest for balance is the fact that we often fail miserably. While we understand the value of having an evenhanded life, our hearts often take one big piece of something we like, rather than cutting all the slices evenly.

Picture this: A man stands in front of you. His upper body resembles Arnold Schwarzenegger's in his *Terminator* days, full of muscle, toned and bronzed, but his lower body seems emaciated like Popeye's Olive Oyl after months of dieting. The guy has focused too much on one part of himself and ignored the rest of himself.

In our lives, we are like the mismatched man, dedicating the lion's share of our time and attention to the develop-ment of one area and ultimately ignoring the others.

This is key for those of us who seek to maximize the effec-tiveness of each day. Our temptation is to dedicate every waking moment toward a goal—finishing a novel, earning a degree, losing that gut, or attracting the opposite sex—but too much focus can have a negative effect. Without a break and restoration, we stop seeing things clearly, we pursue without purpose, and we have problems stepping back to see the bigger picture. When we want something the most, we are often better served by seeking a more balanced approach to life, mixing recreation, exercise, and other activities into our daily routine so that we can move toward our heart's desires renewed and intentional.

One of my favorite stories about balance is from Reverend Albert B. Cleage, Jr. Members of his congregation often asked for advice on how to deal with a pressing life issue. Rather than give them a step-by-step plan or Bible verses on endurance, Reverend Cleage told them to take a nap. As you can imagine, his congregants were confused by this advice, unsure why he would give such a seemingly flippant response to their sincere pleas for guidance. In fact, Cleage wasn't being flippant or demeaning. He recognized that overwork, stress, and worry are culprits that throw us out of balance. Once we lose balance, everything becomes a struggle. We move from places of harmony to places of strain. Cleage was trying to tell his congregation that their overburdened bodies needed to rest so they could refuel and refocus. Then they would clearly view their situations and stay true to their purpose.

Many of us could use the same prescription. We toil and worry away to a point where we are always busy but rarely productive. Others of us have the opposite symptoms: We spend our days perfecting the art of doing nothing. Either way, a huge shift in lifestyle needs to take place.

Establishing a Solid Foundation

Many try to get their life in balance via a day planner. They think about how they're going to distribute all of their activities across the calendar page, fitting in family, church, friends, professional life, and personal desires. They believe balance means learning how to make the seesaw even, when balance is defining your core. Before you can start allotting minutes and efforts to anything, you have to develop the solid core that will guide and center all of your plans.

The core concept is very important in physical health. The core controls the entire body. It's made up of nearly thirty muscles that wrap around the middle of the body. Your arms and your legs are an extension of its power and control. Your core serves as the bridge over which everything meets, passes, and moves. If the core is not clearly defined and strong, everything else will suffer as a result.

In order for you to have a balanced and purpose-reflective life, you have to have a strong spiritual core. That core is God.

One of my favorite verses has always been Matthew 6:33: "But seek first his kingdom and his righteousness and all these things will be given to you as well." Before all things and above all things, we must seek God. We must make him our center, our core. If we pursue His truth, everything else will fall into its right and perfect place. Everything else will come into balance.

Self-Discipline

Maintenance of our core requires a hefty dose of self-discipline. Self-discipline is the main ingredient that allows us to allot our 86400 deliberately and intentionally focus on our purpose. Self-discipline allows us to dedicate ourselves to our choices.

Similar to dedication, which we discussed in the previous chapter, balance helps us recognize and act upon our life priorities. The overworked and overcommitted need to learn to relax, to say "No!"—to undercommit so they can overdeliver. The lazy need to set daily goals that apply their time to growing their imprint on the world. Find a hobby. Apply to at least one job a week. Start a gym regimen. Eat healthier meals. Whatever changes you need to make in your life, stick to them. Make a promise to yourself and have the willpower to keep it.

The Bible encourages us to seek a disciplined diversity in who we are and what we pursue, so that we might become the best version of ourselves. The word that repeatedly appears throughout the text is *self-controlled*. "Therefore, prepare your minds for action; be self-controlled; set your hope fully on the grace to be given you when Jesus Christ is revealed. As obedient children, do not conform to the evil desires you had when you lived in ignorance" (I Pet. 1:13–14). God knows humankind well. Rarely are we composed. We are passionate and prone to anger. We are selfish and ego-driven. We are jealous, excited, curious, and eager. Often we act too quickly out of those feelings.

Look at this in terms of a tightrope walker. If he were to step out onto a rope seeking balance, do you think he would make a running head start, bounding with electricity all the way? Or would he come steadily and intentionally— with self-control?

As we full-of-life, full-of-feeling, full-of-crazy-energy human beings seek balance, we need to take a cue from the tightrope walker, and, more importantly, from the Bible. No wonder God hammers home the term *self-control* so frequently. We are walking a fine line, and it would be so easy to stray from it and fall. Daily, we must abide by and trust in

His will and move forward with the patience and intention required to stay on the rope.

86400 Adviser: Sherri Shepherd—Balance

Sherri Shepherd's love for her son is one of the main reasons she strives for balance in her life as an Emmy Award–winning comedienne and actress and co-host of *The View*. Her purpose is providing for his well-being and development. Her day begins and ends with him. Even her voice eases into a soft, innocent, and child-like mode when she speaks about her son, Jeffrey Charles.

"It just seems like yesterday my son was born prematurely with all of these things the doctors said was wrong with him," she said. "And now he is five years old, and my son is doing everything they said he would not be able to do."

He was born at five and half months' gestation with little hope of having a "normal" childhood. "They said that my son would never be able to jump, walk, or run; that he would be confined to a wheelchair. So when I look at my baby, I'm so thankful of where God brought my son against all odds. I thank Him for the supernatural miracle in my son's life."

Shepherd's morning ritual demonstrates her commitment to balancing her life—with balance that puts God first but makes her son a priority. Prayer is the first order of her day. Spending time with her son is a close second. "I turn over and I look outside my window at the sky and I say, 'Thank you, Lord,' then I get into prayer," said Sherri. "But usually somewhere in the middle of it, I hear 'Mommy, Mommy, Mommy.' Then I go into my son's room, and I lie in bed with

him. We just look at each other and we talk. So really, my day
starts with God and my son. If I don't start it off with asking
God to order my steps, I'm so out of it that it is hard to catch
up. So I would never give up my morning prayers."

Prayer centers her and puts her on the right path for the
day. "When I don't pray in the morning, it's all off track," she
explained. "It's off at *The View*, and Whoopi will look at me
and say, 'I don't know what just came out of your mouth.'"

As a divorced mother with a busy and demanding career,
she finds that balance is everything. "As long as my son is
number one, anything that takes away from me being or
doing things with my son, I can't do it," she said. "I have
to have balance where he knows that at night, Mommy is
going to read a bedtime story with me, we brush our teeth
and we get on our knees and we say, 'Thank you, Lord,' and
Mommy tucks me in. So without balance all that falls by
the wayside."

Shepherd attributes her success to her faith in God and
encouragement from family. She grew up in a Chicago sub-
urb with her parents and two sisters. A self-described "class
clown" who always wanted a performing career, she moved
to Los Angeles as a teenager. Later, she toiled for years as a
legal secretary while performing stand-up comedy at night.
That commitment paved the way for her first big break on
a television comedy. She made numerous appearances on
shows before getting her series, *Sherri*, on the Lifetime
Network, in 2009.

Shepherd is straightforward in how she deals with balance and making the most out of her 86400. "It is important to be conscious of your 86400 because you can't get it
back," she said. "You know my weekends are my down days,
when I don't want to do anything, and when I don't do

anything—and you can't get that time back—then I get hit with it on the back end and I'm out of whack."

At forty-three, Sherri has been on *The View* for three years and is acutely aware of the passage of time. "I remember when I started; it seems like it was just last Tuesday," she said. "Where did this time go? It just scares me sometimes. Time waits for no one. My son will be walking down the aisle before I know it. And I'm so conscious of that time, that 86400."

Aging makes it more crucial to live a balanced life, which for Shepherd includes eating right, exercising, resting, and praying. "I'm here eating a salad not because I want to, but you've got to be conscious of how you spend your time and what you spend it doing," she said. "And if you don't eat right or take care of yourself, you will spend your precious 86400 in a sickbed without the ability to enjoy your 86400.

"I tell my girlfriends that at my age now, I realize that I have to go work out," she said. "No more 'I'll do it next Tuesday.' Heck! You must work out, 'cause now your bones are fusing together—I'm leaving a party walking out in my high heels. I'm saying, Good-bye, everybody. I don't trip in my heels. I'm tripping because my knees just gave out. Time passes, and now it is not about, 'Oh, I want to look cute or fit in a bathing suit.' No, I just want to be alive!"

Shepherd is a diabetic who must adhere to a strict diet and health regimen to keep the disease under control. "Diabetes runs in our family, and stress makes it worse," she said. "So when I'm out of balance my diabetes is out of balance as well."

When she is not living in balance, she said her body also has other ways of telling her. "I get really bad headaches, these migraines, and my head feels like it is in a vise," she said. "My thoughts don't come as easily as they should; and I feel real zoned out." To get back on track, she said she has "to just stop, be conscious of what is going on, take a minute or two, sometimes pray on it. You know, just regroup."

Once she regains balance, she has found that giving herself permission to say no is a powerful tool for managing her 86400. "At this point in my life I have to really prioritize," she said, "and *no* is a beautiful word to me, that wonderful word I discovered: No! You can't survive by being all things to all people. Sometimes you just have to say no."

Shepherd, who published an autobiography in 2009, *Permission Slips: Every Woman's Guide to Giving Herself a Break* (Grand Central Publishing), gives herself permission to say no to the things that would pull her away from her purpose and priorities. "Being balanced helps you to manage your time because being balanced helps you to put everything into perspective," she said. "You don't have to chase stuff. You know what to say no to. You are also able to go ahead and take the risk and just do it.

"You don't have to stress, and that helps to put you in a space to be thankful," she said. "So being balanced cuts out a lot of rushed, bad decisions. It saves your time, because you don't have to double back and fix things you rushed into."

In fact, when we first spoke by telephone for our interview, Shepherd abruptly ended it and asked to reschedule, explaining that she felt unprepared at that moment and wanted to give the 86400 concept more careful thought before speaking about it. "Let me regroup and get my thoughts together," she said. "I apologize, but I want to answer with clarity and I want to give you what you need." The situation did not feel right, and she knew enough to say no.

"I don't like to be unprepared," she explained the next time we spoke. "I don't like having to apologize because I'm not prepared—that makes me even more crazy. Then I'm irritated and whoever is closest to me is going to get it. Then I feel bad because I got irritated. Then I've got to go and pray, because I said something to somebody that I regret thirty seconds later."

That, too, is about balance. "Being unbalanced can cause a snowball effect," she continued. "When I'm unbalanced I just have to stop and acknowledge what is going on, get to the truth of the situation."

Balance has allowed her to excel as an actress, author, comedian, and mother. "To me, if you are able to give a little bit of yourself to a few different things without feeling like everything is going to come crashing down on you, and without going through things all stressed out, that's balance," Shepherd said. "When you are balanced, things feel right. There is peacefulness."

For those who cannot seem to find balance, Shepherd prescribes two Scriptures:

Proverbs 3:5–6

5 Trust in the LORD with all your heart and lean not on your own understanding;
6 in all your ways acknowledge him, and he will make your paths straight.

Philippians 4:6–7

6 Do not be anxious about anything, but in everything, by prayer and petition, with thanksgiving, present your requests to God.

7 And the peace of God, which transcends all understanding, will guard your hearts and your minds in
Christ Jesus.

"Coming from a spiritual perspective, I would say just
stop, get on your knees and pray, and ask God to give you
wisdom and show you the way to go," she said. "With that,
when things are bad you will be able to see the light at the
end of the tunnel."

Keep going toward that light and keep getting back up if
you stumble, she advises. "No matter how many times you
fall," she said, "as long as you can get up, if you can breathe,
and you are not dead, there is hope. Each day, each 86400
that I have, I get up and say, 'Thank you, God, for giving me
another chance to get this 86400 right.' My word of encouragement is, If your heart is still beating, there is hope."

By taking the time to connect with her God, nurture her
son, eat healthy food, and exercise, Sherri creates balance. The
time she spends working is magnified in its effectiveness.

"I don't want my baby to say, 'I'm choosing not to go to
college because I got to stay home and change my mommy's bandages,' or 'I got to be there to help her get out of
the wheelchair.' I don't want that to be how my child has to
spend his 86400 seconds."

We often look upon prayer and meditation time, exercise,
and other balancing opportunities as intrusions into our
precious work time. However, the opposite is true. In committing to the principle of balance, we experience an expo-
nential infusion of purpose. As a reminder to maintain
balance, Shepherd thinks of her son. Her ability to maintain
balance allows her to give him the quality of life and the
future he deserves.

Your Next 600 Seconds

Devote your next 600 seconds to picturing what a balanced life would look like for you. Is yours already in balance? Do you know someone who seems to balance everything well? Consider again the image of a tightrope walker. Stranded above the ground on a thin string, every move he makes has to be intentional. If he were to lean too heavily to the left, right, front, or back, he would topple and fall, never to arrive at his destination. For the tightrope walker, balance isn't mere advice. It's essential for survival.

Put yourself in the tightrope walker's position. The wire is life, and your body represents all the different items you are trying to balance: your job, your family, your dreams, your spirituality, your school. If you were to get on the tightrope now, would you stay balanced or does anything make you top-heavy? How can you rebalance the different areas of your life so you can most effectively walk the tightrope? Think of ways you could achieve more balance. What would you add? What would you subtract?

Seconds for the Spirit

> *"Be very careful, then, how you live—not as unwise but as wise, making the most of every opportunity, because the days are evil. Therefore do not be foolish, but understand what the LORD'S will is"* *(Eph. 5:15–17).*

5

Imagination:
The Dream Maker

*Fairy tales are more than true: not because
they tell us that dragons exist, but because they
tell us dragons can be beaten.*
—G. K. Chesterton

I am an eater, a "foodie." I find a deep satisfaction in my meals, and food fascinates me. According to the *Webster's New World College Dictionary*, a *foodie* is "a person having an enthusiastic interest in the preparation and consumption of fine foods." I don't like to put a label on my passion for food. I just like to eat. I'm a picky eater who enjoys cooking as well as consuming delicious food.

I also love finding interesting restaurants around the world, especially those unknown to many. On the Food Network's *Diners, Drive-ins and Dives*, host Guy Fieri's mission is to find those out-of-the-way, hole-in-the-wall places that serve food fit for kings and queens. Fieri gets excited when he finds one of those small and uncelebrated restaurants. I am the same way. One of my favorite desserts is Key lime pie. I call myself a Key lime pie connoisseur. As I travel the world, I am always in search of the best version. I have found some gems that have become regular stops for me. The creative twists some of the best chefs have taken with this dessert fascinate me. It's imagination at its edible best.

When you let your imagination roam free, you can discover your own passion and purpose, and those discoveries can take you places you would never have thought possible. Let your imagination have its way regularly.

Imagination is the doorway to purpose. Looking at life through our creative eyes, we can see what's hidden from others and even from ourselves. We can discern our best self, our deepest passions, our reason for being. Imagination takes you places your thoughts, ideas, mind, and heart would normally dare not venture. It is in those places, just off the beaten path, that we can experience our greatest inner revelations.

We are Called to Something Bigger

Do you remember elementary school, complete with that obese yellow bus arriving early in the morning before the rooster crowed, crossing guards who had an inexplicable attachment to their whistles, and cafeteria lunches served on plastic trays with miniature cartons of chocolate milk? Surely you remember the books, the bullies, and the school spelling bees where nervous children clicked their heels across the gymnasium floor only to reach the podium and misspell words like *possum* or *chili*.

More than any of those things, I remember the science fair—that once-a-year event where kids were asked to re-create Earth's catastrophes or come up with the craziest inventions. Boys and girls wobbled down the hallways carrying plywood topped with exploding Play-Doh volcanoes. Toothpaste shot out of a malfunctioning, futuristic teeth-cleansing mechanism. I can remember my science projects as if I had made them yesterday. The night before the science fair, I sat at the kitchen table with my mom and dad connecting wires, trying to get the lightbulb, a critical part of my science project on electricity, to light up.

The science fair is one of the best parts of elementary school. It teaches eight-, nine-, and ten-year-olds that it's essential to explore, to question, to try again, again, and again until the big idea becomes the big reality.

Larry Page and Sergey Brin sound like the names of two guys you would invite over to watch the Super Bowl and share a pot of gumbo, but Larry and Sergey aren't average. They're the guys who met at Stanford when Larry was twenty-two and Sergey was twenty-one, hit it off, collaborated on an idea, and created Google, according to www.google.com's list of corporate milestones. I wonder what they did for science fair projects?

All Google engineers are encouraged to take one day out of their week, equivalent to 20 percent of their time, and focus on a project that has piqued their interest, according to a *New York Times* article, "The Google Way: Give Engineers Room," by Bharat Mediratta, as told to Julie Bick (October 21, 2007).

It doesn't matter if it's on their to-do list, or if it's even been requested. Google just decided it was a good company policy to let the pups out of their cage to see what they could dig up. It's no surprise that 50 percent of Google's new products and services, such as Gmail, Google News,

Orkut, and AdSense, all came from this program called Innovation Time Off.

In Jerry de Jaager and Jim Ericson's book *See New Now: New Lenses for Leadership and Life* (Bergen Publishing, 2009), they write, "A study of the top fifty game-changing innovations over a hundred-year period showed that nearly 80 percent of those innovations were sparked by someone whose primary expertise was outside the field in which the innovation breakthrough took place."

We all excel most when our interest is sincere and passionate, when we are inquisitive. As we dig deeper with our questions and open up our imaginations, the chance of a harebrained notion becoming the next big idea is exponentially higher. So are the chances of an unfulfilled and unproductive life becoming one of purpose and power. We grow in direct proportion to the scope, grandeur, and audacity of our imagination.

Consider what God has planned for your life. Can you envision a reality that gets your heart racing and bears witness that "the glory of God is man fully alive," as the Roman Catholic Saint Irenaeus wrote? Imagination is God's gift to us to explore what He has created. Imagination allows us to plug into divine purpose. The problem is that, for most of us, imagination is one of the least used of all God's gifts. It is said that up to 80 percent of what humans do on a daily basis is out of habit—rote, mechanical, programmed, conditioned, unimaginative, nonthinking, uninspired, robotic routine. Also factor in that most of us sleep 20 to 33 percent of each day, and that leaves us little time to use our imaginations. No wonder we find it hard to live effective, intention-filled lives. We're running on automatic pilot!

Imagination, creativity, and spontaneity are critical to

discovering and deploying your divine purpose. Romans 12:6–8 reads, "We have different gifts, according to the grace given us. If a man's gift is prophesying, let him use it in proportion to his faith. If it is serving, let him serve; if it is teaching, let him teach; if it is encouraging, let him encourage; if it is contributing to the needs of others, let him give generously; if it is leadership, let him govern diligently; if it is showing mercy, let him do it cheerfully."

We are created with specific gifts, and those gifts and callings are intertwined deeply into our dreams. With imagination, we seek out our heart's calling and thereby find the life God intends for us. Worlds to explore await us if we but give ourselves permission to use our imaginations in our daily 86400 seconds.

Still to Come

When my adopted brother, Tyrone, was five years old, he was classified as having a learning disability. It was harsh news, but my parents never gave up. They found a school in Lafayette, Louisiana, that catered to special-needs children. Unfortunately, the waiting list to enroll in the school was long. It could be months or years before he could attend. Never giving up, my mom asked if any school in Houston where I lived would be appropriate for him to attend until an opening was available at the school in Lafayette. I was an instructional supervisor at the time in the Houston Independent School District, and I knew the perfect school for him, Nat Q. Henderson Elementary. We completed all the paperwork and at the beginning of the school year, Tyrone moved in with my husband and me. I was in my early twenties, and I thought handling a five-year-old was going to be a breeze. Wishful thinking. After the first week I wanted to ship him back to my mom and dad. I knew they missed him dearly and would have happily picked him up at the UPS or FedEx store. It was rough. He hated school. It was a struggle getting him up in the morning and making him eat his breakfast. After that, we had to drag him to the car, and then drag him all the way to his class each morning. Luckily, he had a no-nonsense teacher who took over from there.

What could I do to get him to like school? I searched and searched, thought and thought. My imagination cap went on one day. Tyrone loved sports: basketball, football, and baseball—you name it. I made up a couple of stories about a rooster that loved sports too. I called him Rooster Roux, but later I changed the name to Roopster Roux, because Tyrone had trouble saying "Rooster." He would always call him Roopster. I started telling these stories about Roopster to Tyrone during dinner and sometimes in the car on the way to Tyrone's school. Roopster Roux was the best at every sport, I would tell him, but there was a catch. He loved to go to school and he loved to read. He loved reading so much that he would use his reading abilities to defeat the bad guys and win all the games he played. The stories helped me manage Tyrone a little better.

After the winter break there was an opening at the school in Louisiana, so Tyrone was back with my mom and dad after Christmas. We bypassed FedEx and UPS and drove him home to my parents. I am proud to say that with time and patience, Tyrone learned to read, and is doing well living with my mom in Louisiana. Years later, those stories about Roopster Roux became my first children's book series, *The*

Adventures of Roopster Roux (Pelican, 1998). That gift of imagination opened up a world of opportunities for me. I've been blessed to continue to write, work with children, and actively live on purpose, making the most of my 86400.

Na'vi hasn't been a word for very long. It became familiar to me in 2009 after spending 150 minutes watching massive blue aliens dance across a big screen. For James Cameron, Na'vi has been a word since 1994. According to various articles, he spent two weeks, eighty pages, and who knows how many cups of coffee jotting down his ideas for *Avatar*. At the time, he was putting the finishing touches on a little flick called *Titanic* and was looking for what was next. His idea: synthetic actors in a brand-new world. He toyed with the idea then, but inevitably tucked it away. His reasoning: Technology hadn't caught up with his vision. It wouldn't be until December 2009, fifteen years later, that the ideas in his head would show up in front of our eyes.

I hear that story and I wonder, How did the man have the patience? Anytime I get a good idea, I want to carry it out at that moment. I want to take advantage of it immediately. I don't want to let it mull or ripen, processes that should be left to beverages and fruits. Yet James Cameron sat on his grand vision for over a decade. He put it in a drawer and moved on, waiting for the time when the idea was ready, rather than when he *wanted* it to be ready.

Where did he come up with Pandora and Na'vi, the unbelievably beautiful bounding blue aliens? A sense of miraculous wonder and creativity infuses every pixel on that screen. James Cameron didn't settle for anything ordinary. He didn't adapt and blend and create a hodgepodge of every-thing we've all seen before. He settled into a conversation with his imagination and let it work. Because of his grand escapade into the mind's eye, millions of us stood in line to wear awkward 3-D glasses and have our minds wowed.

We got to experience the beauty of creativity because Cameron is living his purpose—conveying moving and memorable stories via the silver screen that speak to issues greater than money or fame, such issues as love, honor, integrity, and commitment. *Avatar* has been lauded because it's the first of its kind. People use words like *groundbreaking* and *revolutionary* to describe it.

Everything ever made, produced, or invented first existed as an idea born of someone's imagination. Everything, at some point, had to be "the first." What James Cameron did is remarkable, but we are all capable of using the initial component: imagination. We are all equipped with the potential to believe in more. We're not just capable. We're called to use our mind's eye to make the most of our God-given time. It's part of God's great composition.

Picture something a little absurd. Take your town or your neighborhood and put it in a snow globe. Yes, put your house, your yard, your grocery store, your church, your school, your workplace, and yourself all in the snow globe. Seal it up and put it on a shelf.

Living inside that snow globe, most days, you're a pretty happy camper. You pluck along, you do your routine, and you are content, but then one day, you decide you want to take a long walk. You inevitably come to the edge of the snow globe. You put your face up to the glass and cup your hands around your eyes to see better. Do you know what you see? An entire row of other snow-globe villages sitting on the shelf: Chicago and Boston. Des Moines and Albuquerque. Denver and San Francisco. They are all there in the rows, the people in them living their unique lives, very different, it appears, from the one in your snow globe. When you walk back to your house that night, you lie down in bed and you start thinking about all the other snow-globe villages. You realize how many worlds are out there! Just then, as your mind is churning, something crazy happens. When you start believing in the excitement and potential of the things you haven't seen, the top of the snow globe begins to open and you are able, for the first time in your life, to go places you've never gone before.

We have to tap into our imaginations to grow in our potential and our purpose. We have to believe in impossibilities. We must seek what others naysay. Maximizing the productivity of each moment demands our minds. It's the first critical step to producing anything, and its power is limitless because it is confined only by the boundaries of our creativity.

IMAGINATION

My cousin Twiler Portis and I grew up together in Louisiana, spending holidays and family reunions together. Twiler is a sought-after inspirational/motivational speaker who travels the world showing couples and families how they can get on the fast track to true health, wealth, and happiness. She is well known as the host of her morning inspirational call, a teleconference to which people from around the world call in to hear and share positive business practices. I am very proud of my cousin and her husband for the many people they are helping to get on track and to live life on purpose. I loved chatting with her about how she uses her imagination to manage her 86400.

Twiler Portis
Founder of Portis Industries, entrepreneur, and inspirational speaker.

A formal definition of "imagination" would be the power to call up mental images. When I think about imagination, I think about the power of the mind—how you see things. Imagination is your ability to bring something forward or to life through your thought process.

I always enjoyed speaking, encouraging and inspiring others. As a little girl, I would imagine myself speaking to large crowds of people, thousands, if you will. I worked on that, never stopped working on my speaking skills. When I went on to college, my major was telecommunications. I moved on from there to thinking that I wanted to be a news anchor. When I finally started to see it coming to fruition is when I started my morning inspirational teleconference calls. Little did I know that I was going to end up speaking to thousands of individuals from all over the country.

I started to imagine that I would be speaking to thousands when I was very young, and it came into being as an adult. My morning inspirational call is about my love for people and inspiring people to tap into what they already have to be successful. I started it with small testimonies. Five to six people would get on the call and share experiences and the principles they used to have a healthier life, a wealthier life. Now that simple morning call has grown to thousands. Because I'm going to be talking to those people first thing in the morning, I get up a little before my inspirational call, and I have my private time with my Savior, and I roll right into the inspirational call. The vast majority of what I do during the day is encouraging people to move to the next level, laying out game plans to help them. I think that if you are goal oriented, really working business a lot, you really have to find some balance in there, and in your 86400 you have to have balance with business, family, and spirituality.

I have always aligned myself with individuals who will stretch me. I heard my pastor say a while back that if you are the sharpest knife in the drawer, you need to jump into a new drawer. I align myself with people who are smart, who are successful, and who are wiser than me. It allows me to imagine that if I put those principles—the ones that help them reach that level of success—into place, I would have some of those same successes.

When asked who is the most imaginative person I know, I would say Walt Disney is that person for me. You know, he was fired from his job at a newspaper. They said he lacked imagination. Now can you imagine that? Once the paper fired him, he began to work on theme parks and the various characters. When the theme park opened, [someone] interviewed his wife and said to her, "Isn't it a shame that he did not get to see the park open?" Her response was, "If he had not *seen* it, you would not be seeing it today." The man just had incredible imagination. He showed you how to let your imagination be free and not be afraid to make mistakes—to be bold in that whole process. To me, he is an imaginative thinker.

I believe that people who are lost or struggling have not made the decision to not be lost or struggling. God has given us all a share, and the only difference between a struggling person and someone who is not struggling is the decision to want more. I tell people to find someone who is doing it and copy them. I believe that everyone has the potential to win. Lots of times, the struggling person is walking alongside the wrong people. They don't have the right mentor or the right person to follow, or they are listening to someone who is struggling or someone who is lost. Having a mentor who is right there with you is great, an ideal situation. But if you don't have that person it is okay to follow someone from afar. I've done both—up close and from afar. It is okay to look at a successful person on TV, radio. You can follow people who are not in your immediate circle. Read, get a DVD, a CD, listen to information that will empower you, impact you. I know many people who were struggling, and they made a decision to change. God put people in your way with power and influence to help you—you have to want it.

I always imagine that if I stay diligent, focused, and intentional about the things I have to do during the course of that day, I will be successful. Each day that I awake, I'm constantly thinking and saying, "Imagine this! What if that?" My thinking, my imagination, within the course of the day helps me to believe in the possibilities. Imagine if I get this done! Imagine the time I will have for the rest of the day to do whatever. Sometimes just thinking about or imagining the rewards that you garner if certain things are accomplished helps you to focus and want to get it done within a certain time frame. I realize that some days don't go as planned, but you still have to plan your time wisely. I always imagine if I can just get it done, it will take my family to new levels.

When I'm working on something in business, I get totally involved. What I found is that when you are totally involved and passionate about something, business or personal, you start imagining the possibilities of what can happen, and all the great things start to happen. I think creativity, imagination, they both work hand and hand.

Your time is valuable. Once it is gone, it is gone forever. God has given me this time, and what I do with it is my gift back to Him. You really should want to give God a good gift. I think that every day we should be conscious of the time He has given us. When it is all said and done, He is the reason that we have it in the first place. So we need to use it very wisely.

Making Good on God and the Rabbit Hole

At this point, you may be thinking, I don't have room for imagination. I go to work. I cook dinner. I pay the bills. I love my family.

Sometimes, as responsible adults, we trick ourselves into believing that to have any dream or fantasy means we aren't acting our age. But what if "being responsible" was the least responsible thing you could actually do? What if our calling was one of creativity? Our minds need to be a bit acrobatic.

One of the most imaginative individuals in the world is Stevie Wonder. Not only is he an accomplished pianist, he is a master harmonica player, master drummer, and superior vocalist. Though he's physically blind, Wonder possesses an inner vision (imagination) that allows him to read the feelings and moods of individuals, communities, and whole nations and meld his music to these feelings in a socially relevant and inspiring way. The countless awards Wonder has won and accolades he has garnered pale in comparison to his impact on the hearts and minds of those moved by his music.

Jesus scolded the religious leadership of his day for not possessing inner vision. Jesus was frustrated because those individuals charged with the spiritual health of a nation could read the signs and predict the weather but could not read the signs of the times; they lacked the vision and imagination to see future possibilities.

Though frustrated, Jesus knew that not everyone was open to the power of the imagination. That is why He told His Disciples, "But blessed are your eyes because they see, and your ears because they hear. For I tell you the truth, many prophets and righteous men longed to see what you see but did not see it, and to hear what you hear but did not hear it" (Matt. 13:16–17).

Throughout the Bible, in this story, as in others, God calls His followers to believe what society would scream is impossible. In Luke 8 is the story of a man named Jairus and his twelve-year-old daughter, who is dying. While Jesus was speaking, a ruler in the synagogue approached the father, saying, "Your daughter is dead. Don't bother the teacher anymore." But hearing this, Jesus replied, "Don't be afraid; just believe and she will be healed" (Luke 8:49–50).

There, too, is the story of Jesus feeding the 5000. The crowd that had gathered to hear Him speak was huge, it was late, and they were in a remote area. When Jesus told His Disciples to feed the people, His Disciples said, "That would take eight months of a man's wages! Are we to go and spend that much on bread and give it to them to eat?" But Jesus assured them and they took five loaves and two fish and fed the whole of the people (Mark 6:30–44).

The stories in the Bible demonstrate God's hope that we will believe in things bigger than ourselves. When we are able to let down our tendencies to "rationalize" and "be practical," when we open our minds to the idea that "Yes, truly this can happen!" the glory of God is waiting for us. Our purpose, our destiny, our higher calling is before us. We have to give ourselves permission to see it. All we have to do is believe.

86400 Adviser: Dennis Devorick— Imagination

The Reverend Dennis Devorick, a United Methodist minister and principal of an elementary school in a small city in

Western Pennsylvania, has a coffee mug a student gave him the first year he taught school. It has an image of the Norman Rockwell painting *The Toy Maker* and these words: *He is the hero of the village, because he works wonders for little boys and girls. He can make a single piece of wood come alive and stir the imagination of any youngster. He is more than a toy maker, he is a dream maker.*

"That has become my goal and my motto," he told me. "I want to be a dream maker."

"Dreamers are the ones who change the world," Devorick said. "The Disneys, the Steve Jobs, and the Bill Gates of the world are the ones who dream about doing things differently." His work at the school, Laurel Elementary in New Castle, Pennsylvania, which lies northwest of Pittsburgh and near the Ohio border, exemplifies the virtue of imagination. "Without imagination, you're stuck in a box," he said. "Imagination, to me, is akin to creativity. It allows you to break with the monotony. When I'm creative, I'm productive. I use my time wisely to stay motivated, reach goals, and help others reach their goals. Without imagination on a daily basis, I would be a robot. I wouldn't get much done. But imagination changes the world. It ignites the best kinds of fires. Without imagination, life would be pretty boring and not much would get done."

His school's theme, "Helping People Here, There and Everywhere," boldly announces his purpose, and everything about his school is impressive—the office personnel, teachers, students, and parents.

"As a principal, a major role is to be a visionary, to dream of a better place," he said. "I convinced the school board to fund a major renovation of our school. I did a kind of

Who Wants to Be a Millionaire–themed presentation, asking, "What will a million dollars do for our school?" His imaginative approach helped to secure the funds to renovate his school.

"When I became the principal of Laurel thirteen years ago, there were no computers in the schools," he recalled. "We added a science lab and a computer lab. We were able to welcome back our special-education program, and, as bizarre as it might sound to say, all of that happened because I had a dream. My imagination led me to think with no boundaries."

He learned to dream and imagine early in life. "Growing up, I played with LEGOs," he said. "The LEGO box said something like *Your imagination is your only limitation.*"

He encourages the staff and the students to use their imaginations as well. "We paint pictures and murals on the wall to encourage kids to dream and use their imagination," he explained. "We create themes and other worlds. We have in drummers from Africa, artists from China, and authors to inspire kids."

Devorick is proud that the students of Laurel Elementary are becoming knowledgeable, responsible, and engaged contributors to an ever-changing global society. After Hurricane Katrina, the students published a book called *A Gift of a Rainbow* through the Every Child an Author program. Copies have been sent to most of the schools hit by Hurricanes Katrina and Rita, to Ronald McDonald Houses in America, and to children in need of hope around the world. The proceeds have helped to support four charities in the New Castle area.

"With Every Child an Author, our kids are becoming published authors," said Devorick, whom I first met when

I visited the school for the program. "They are not just passive listeners. They are actively using their imagination—writing, and then seeing the finished product in book form. All that to help them to overcome prejudices, see the beauty in other people."

Story after story from teachers and parents about Devorick's leadership highlighted his imagination. A guidance counselor recalled that during Devorick's first weeks as Laurel's principal, he let his staff know that changes would be made and that the process would not necessarily be smooth. However, he assured them that when you do the right thing with good intentions, things would go in the right direction. To demonstrate this point at a faculty meeting, he stood on his head and ate a sandwich. His point was that God has so fearfully and wonderfully made us that even though he was standing on his head, his sandwich would go in the right direction: to his stomach.

As Reverend Devorick, pastor of United Methodist churches in the nearby towns of Elkton and Negley, Ohio, he relies heavily upon imagination in his Sunday sermons and believes Christians could benefit from imagination every day of the week. "Imagination helps me help people see the world differently, ultimately motivating them to effectively accomplish goals," he said. "In order to be a Christian, you need to see the world beyond your senses. You need to experience what you can't see. It's a gift of the spirit to be imaginative."

Devorick says his ideas often come during the middle of the night, prompting him to awake and write them down in his journal. "You never know when a beautiful, bold idea will approach you," he said. "Your mind is always active. Be ready for it."

Devorick uses his God-given 86400 effectively to live his purpose of making a difference in the lives of many. Beginning each day in prayer, Devorick uses every available second, whether in the shower or during his thirty-minute commute from Columbiana, Ohio, to school, to think, reflect, and organize his day. "Time has limits; don't waste it," said Devorick. "You have to realize that every day is a gift. A sign in his car reads, "I refuse to grow up."

Devorick, who has been a participant in Oprah Winfrey's O Ambassadors program, helping to build schools in underprivileged countries, knows from experience that dreams require tangible follow-through.

"When we helped build the schools in Africa, we had to first imagine it," he recalled. "Then we had to take that and put it into action to make what we imagined really happen. Imagination gives you freedom to have no boundaries of where you go."

Whether encouraging his students at school or inspiring his congregants at church, Pastor Devorick prescribes heavy doses of imagination. "Stay positive, dream, be in prayer, and seek God's guidance and direction," he said.

To use one's 86400 effectively and fulfill one's purpose, the dreamer then has to get up off his or her knees and work. "God speaks to us in our prayers, and God puts those thoughts, dreams, imagination, into us that enable us to act on them," he said. "Everything that you imagine may not be realistic, but you can't spend your life imagining and not doing," he concluded. "Let your imagination help you to look at different possibilities and for ways of doing things. Then from there you have to take action."

Your Next 600 Seconds

Devote your next 600 seconds to thinking of ways you can use your imagination in every area of your life to use your 86400 to the fullest. Imagine several alternatives for your future. Apply your creativity to planning how you would achieve each outcome for your life. Imagine how your life might be affected if you changed only one thing—your neighborhood, your job, or your exercise routine, for instance.

Seconds for the Spirit

> *"Where there is no vision, the people perish"* (Prov. 29:18 *KJV*).

6

Thankfulness: Stop the Pity Party

*I thank God for my handicaps, for, through them,
I have found myself, my work, and my God.*
—Helen Keller

I grew up with a solid foundation from the teachings in the Bible. I had great examples from my parents, grandmother, nuns, priests, and preachers of how to live in thanksgiving. I prayed in school, after school, in Sunday school, and in Baptist Training Union (BTU), and attended church twice on Sunday.

As I grew up and became very busy, however, I strayed from the daily practice of prayer and giving thanks to God. Part of my journey back began, as I mentioned previously, when I read *The One Year Bible*. Reading it sparked my interest, but it also shook my confidence. I questioned my ability to pray in the reflective and effective manner that I learned so well as a child. For me, the adage "Once you learn how to ride a bike you never forget" did not apply.

When I began my trek toward reclaiming my personal

relationship with God, for some odd reason I thought I needed an elaborate setup to give thanks to my Lord for all my blessings. I bought a little table and rimmed it with candles; I burned incense and sat on an Egyptian pillow as I recited the prayers I'd learned as a child and new ones I read in *The One Year Bible*. Still, I didn't feel I was doing it right. When I tried to pray and thank God for leading me back to him, I felt so insincere. It was not until I came in one day, from a wearying fifteen-plus-hour flight from Angola to Houston, that I experienced a breakthrough.

I plopped down on my sofa, kicked off my heels, and said aloud, "Thank you, God, for getting me back here safe." It came out so naturally. I literally felt chills after saying that. It was an "ah-ha" moment for me. All my Bible reading and formal prayer rituals had failed to put me in that comfort zone with God. That simple "Thank you, God" granted me inner peace.

Not long after that, I traveled to Atlanta for an education conference. I arrived at the airport early for my flight back to Houston. I was browsing through the airport bookstore when I stumbled upon and purchased a small, purple paperback book full of prayers for just about every occasion. It included a prayer titled "The Joy of the Lord" that stood out for me, spoke to my spirit, and released my insecurities. I felt like I had written it myself. I memorized it and recited it daily. I still do.

It was such a powerful book that I had to bless others with it. That Christmas I ordered fifteen copies directly from the publisher. (I was thankful to get that order in because shortly after that the book went out of print and is no longer being sold.) I wrote special sayings in each of them for my family and closest friends. To this day, I get a warm, fuzzy feeling when I see the book at my aunt Helen's bedside or happen upon my mother reading it. You can see that they read their little purple books as often as I read mine. The wear and tear on their copies is quite obvious. What was most special to me were the visits with my father in the hospital during the last year of his life. He was in and out of the hospital, and during every stay his little purple book of prayers remained right next to him, along with his Bible. Actually, the book was often in the bed with him, as he would regularly fall asleep reading it. I was amazed that such a simple gift would be the one he cherished most. He loved reading that book so much that I wanted to keep his copy after he passed on. But because he cherished it so much, I placed it right next to him in his final resting place so that he would never be without it. I'm overwhelmed with tears of thankfulness as I write about my dad and that little purple book.

During difficult times, my sadness no longer lingers. I'm getting better at being able to pray through it and push forward, giving thanks for past memories, present moments, and future victories. Thankfulness is the energy that invites positive opportunities and outcomes. Gratitude keeps me mindful of the purpose for which God has placed me here.

A State of Thanksgiving

The art of being thankful keeps your countenance in a good place and your energy alluring. Being thankful wards off negativity the way insect repellent wards off bugs. It invites positive exchanges. Hence, thankfulness is critical to those seeking lives of purpose. Thankfulness facilitates your operation of your purpose. Living each day in a state of thanksgiving gives each of your 86400 seconds more potential because you are a blessing waiting to happen.

I enjoy reading biographies and magazine feature articles, or watching documentaries that focus on people's life journeys. It is amazing how consistently testimonials about thankfulness are given by those who are successful. One after another, they talk about how they were in a bad place emotionally or financially, or how they faced a character-testing hurdle, only to be rescued by their own spirit of thanksgiving. In their trial, the person found something for which to give thanks, and, soon thereafter, solutions once hidden were revealed. Doors thought forever closed opened again. Opportunities believed to be long gone resurfaced or were replaced by even better possibilities.

Thankfulness is one of the greatest transmitters of value. It reminds us of the power of our blessings, the wonder of our grace, the magnificence of God's love. Thankfulness illuminates the passionate leanings of our heart, our purpose.

When I was growing up, my mom would pile servings of food on my plate—particularly vegetables. Steaming sweet peas. Stringy green beans. Baked squash. I would gulp down a bite or two, push the veggies around with my fork, and hope she wouldn't see through my ploy. Like all good mothers, she always did. I couldn't leave the table until I'd cleaned my plate.

I didn't understand her reasoning at the time. Eating vegetables felt like punishment, but she was trying to teach me to value God's provisions.

Thankfulness is, at its core, what happens when we understand the value of what we have. Making the most of our 86400 means we recognize the blessings in our life, and treat them carefully. We are more cognizant of their meaning and the cost for us to possess them.

THANKFULNESS

Elvin Hayes and I met a number of years ago while we were both working on a construction project for our respective companies, and we have remained friends. I regularly meet with him over lunch to discuss mutual business ventures and charitable projects. In addition to being an NBA legend, he is a successful businessman. Through all of his success, he constantly displays his thankfulness for what he has achieved.

Elvin Hayes
NBA Hall of Famer and member of the NBA's 50th Anniversary All-Time Team. He is one of the NBA's Top 50 greatest basketball players.

I start my day by being thankful for knowing where I came from and knowing where I am today and knowing where I'm going. Before I started playing basketball, I had gone barefooted for the first twelve years of my life in Louisiana. My mother could not afford any shoes. I was barefooted summer, winter, and fall, on the pavement and on the gravel.

Then, all of a sudden, someone, when I was in the eighth grade, said that he was going to put me on the basketball team. I had never owned a pair of shoes from the time I was born until then. I had to make a decision. Would I go home or would I go into the bathroom and get two left-footed tennis shoes to put on my feet to start playing basketball? Two left-footed tennis shoes were in the trashcan. To put on those shoes changed the whole course of my life. The thankfulness that I have came from that moment.

When I first got those two left-footed tennis shoes, I put them on my feet, and I was thankful then for the opportunity that the coach gave me to play basketball, not knowing that when he allowed me to put on those two left tennis shoes I would become one of the fifty greatest NBA players, be a Hall of Famer. That's why I'm thankful, from that moment of grace and every one of my moments. Think about what that moment with that coach propelled me to be. If that happened from that one moment early in my life, think about what potential can and did happen from all the moments in my life.

To this day, I am thankful because I know where I came from and how blessed I am. I was thankful that day; ever since then, I look at every day being thankful because of the fact of where I have come from, where I am today, and where I am going. God has blessed me with each day being able to have the strength, the mind, and the focus and the direction and the humbleness to receive blessings and to accept those things that are coming to me.

When I look at life, I see it as a stormy day. It can rain and storm for an hour, and everyone is saying, "This is horrible!" How I look at it is that I know that when the clouds clear out, the sun will shine through. That's the way it is in real life. This is only for a little while.

The Bible says that the trials and tribulations of the righteous are many, but I shall deliver you through them all. ["A righteous man may have many troubles, but the LORD delivers him from them all" (Ps. 34:19).] That is a Scripture I hold dear to me, because I know that I will have difficult times, but I know that the sun is still shining above the difficult times. Tomorrow we will look out after the rain is gone and we will say, "Wow! It is beautiful out here. It is so refreshing!" Difficult times and trials only make us better. They make us better people. They make us stronger people, and this is what the storms in my life have always done for me.

In basketball, when we lost a game, it was not always a loss to me. The loss was a gain because what it did was help me to correct myself in some of the mistakes that I made. It made me a much better player, and if I had not had those difficult times I might not have been a Hall of Fame basketball player or one of the fifty greatest NBA players. Without hard times you can't know good times. Each day I'm steady growing, just as a plant breaks through the soil to get to the sun; bad times to me is steady breaking me through the soil to get me to the good times.

This is the attitude or my approach that keeps me on purpose. My purpose? I'm here to touch a life. As I look at nature, like when God blesses a tree, that tree will let its leaves fall to the ground. They turn into compost, and they fertilize the grass and the trees and bring nourishment to other animals. So many creatures find food and shelter from that tree. So that's touching so many lives.

I feel that the human being is needed the same way, for us to be able to touch another life, to be able to lift another life—as in basketball, not to just take from it, but to be able to give to it. We are able to bring joy or happiness to a person coming to cheer at a game, but not only that, we also are able to open doors, to give to someone to help them grow, to teach a young person to play basketball or be successful. I feel that my job or purpose is to be able to touch another life or soul, as my soul was touched by this coach who tapped me in the eighth grade and put me on the basketball team.

I start each day on my knees. I start with a prayer that God will give me the courage to be able to accomplish and achieve things that are before me, that He might be blessed, that all glory is His and not mine. All the things that I achieve and accomplish through this day are not for my own self but that I will bring glory and honor to Him. At the beginning of each day, I tell myself, "Elvin, you are a tremendous person!" So many times in life you will not get a pat on the back, so I give myself a pat on the back in the morning. I tell myself, "Elvin, you are going to be terrific today! You are going to touch lives. You are going to bless someone's life today." At the end of my day, I tell myself, "Elvin, I'm so proud of you, because you really worked hard. You made the sacrifices and you dedicated yourself to help grow your business and help others to grow their business. I am just so proud of you. You had a terrific day. You are terrific." I end my day that way.

It is extremely important to be conscious of our 86400. Time begins to fly the moment you are born. That needle is ticking. Some people might live an hour, or a few seconds at birth, some might live sixty years or a hundred years, but each one of those seconds is so important, because from one second to the next is not promised to you. You have to take each second and each click of the clock, live it, and try to bless and try to touch others and grow your life to be able to give to the level of success that you desire. Because for every second that you lose, that is something that you can never get back, not one second, half, or fraction.

We have to realize that life—time—is the most precious gift we have. We can't go back and sweep it up. I try to make myself stronger, to make my focus brighter toward the goals I'm trying to achieve in life.

The first bit of advice or encouragement that I give young people trying to navigate their way through life is that first you have to have a goal. The second thing is that you have to have a foundation in life. My mother gave me a foundation of prayer and the Bible.

The next thing I give a person is three words, and if they can incorporate these three in their life, then they will be a success. You have to be able to *work* hard, to *dedicate* yourself, and to make *sacrifices*. If you want to be a great scientist, people will say that that person works hard, is dedicated, and makes sacrifices to accomplish their goals. Of the best student in class, people will say that that person works hard, is dedicated, and makes sacrifices. My mother was great. She sacrificed, worked hard, and dedicated herself to her family. You can't dedicate and not work hard. You can't sacrifice and not dedicate. You can't separate the words. If young people will set a goal and incorporate those three things, they will be successful.

When I incorporated in my young life the principles of working hard, dedication, and sacrifice, those have been my tools for success. I was motivated by the fact that I did not want to be working in the fields and doing the stuff I had to do as a child. To pull away from the life I had as a kid was my driving force, to know where I came from, to want to better myself—my drive to not ever go back to doing what I had to do then.

I came to the University of Houston with a hanger tied around my brown suitcase. My mother gave me seventy-five cents to come to school with. I told my mother that one day I was going to accomplish and achieve certain things in my life. I've been blessed to achieve some of those goals. Each day I try to have done something toward my goals.

I was in the car business for twenty years. They said I would never be successful. I was one of the most successful dealers for twenty years in a row. I take the gifts that I was blessed with to use my seconds wisely. My driving force is that I use "from where I came" as a motivator to keep me going forward. You have to have a reason for doing.

My drive for doing things is I lived in a segregated town, worked in the cornfields and the hay fields, and I had no rights. I had to do what I was told. My driving force was to get away from that. Now I'm in the position to do what I desire. I keep my focus and the same humbleness from that same moment when I put on those two left tennis shoes to play basketball. I was thankful then, and I'm thankful today. Being thankful helps me to stay focused and stay on purpose toward my goals.

Avoiding Veruca Salt Syndrome

There is a reality show called *My Super Sweet Sixteen* in which teenagers get such things as expensive cars and jewelry for their birthdays. Their families rent facilities, hire celebrity acts, and give them hundreds of thousands of dollars' worth of gifts. I am intrigued every time I pause the channel to watch a soon-to-be sixteen-year-old who is flummoxed because she can't be flown to her party in a helicopter. I find it fascinating and equally disheartening that young individuals already feel they deserve so much. Their lavish parties and gifts never seem to be enough. They are modern-day Veruca Salts—wanting more, more, more. (If you are a fan of Willy Wonka, you know Veruca Salt. She is the appallingly greedy, pudgy little princess, the daughter of Henry and Henrietta Salt, who never seems to have enough.)

Most of us are repulsed by the unthankful behavior on *My Super Sweet Sixteen*. For my sixteenth birthday, I had streamers and a tasty cake, a couple of gifts—and that, to me, was a pretty huge deal.

Yet these sixteen-year-olds are us. We severely underestimate the extent of our blessings. We feel entitled. We believe that we "deserve" certain opportunities, rather than that we are blessed with them. We are all very good at taking things for granted. We are not much different from the birthday girl having a pity party over a helicopter ride. In our ingratitude for the blessings we do have, we repel people who can help us live our purpose more fully. Our 86400 seconds get away from us as we sulk.

In the parable of the rich fool in Luke, Jesus says, "Watch

out! Be on your guard against all kinds of greed; a man's life does not consist in the abundance of his possessions" (Luke 12:15).

What conviction. What truth. Yet how quickly we lose sight of that truth. Greed emerges from a lack of thankfulness. It arises when we close our eyes to what is important in God's kingdom, and instead seek things of social or material importance. If we are not continually aware of how blessed we are, we will become Verucas who insist we deserve more, and fill our lives with worldly things that do not reflect our purpose, that sidetrack us from our purpose.

Consider how much more fulfilling your life would be if you filled your 86400s with thankfulness.

Luke 17:11–19 recalls how Jesus heals the ten lepers and only one comes back to thank Him:

11 Now on his way to Jerusalem, Jesus traveled along the border between Samaria and Galilee.

12 As he was going into a village, ten men who had leprosy met him. They stood at a distance

13 and called out in a loud voice, "Jesus, Master, have pity on us!"

14 When he saw them, he said, "Go, show yourselves to the priests." And as they went, they were cleansed.

15 One of them, when he saw he was healed, came back, praising God in a loud voice.

16 He threw himself at Jesus' feet and thanked him—and he was a Samaritan.

17 Jesus asked, "Were not all ten cleansed? Where are the other nine?

18 Was no one found to return and give praise to God except this foreigner?"

19 Then he said to him, "Rise and go; your faith has made you well."

Love for the Sour

Thankfulness isn't simply about being happy with what we have. As Christians, we are also called to be thankful even in difficult situations—giving thanks in all things. When life is hard, when tears are quick, and when pain is ripe, we are told to give glory to God.

Who is thankful for hurt? This is not masochistic thinking. It is a healthy response that relinquishes the idea that we know best and affirms that God is always in control. When we are able to believe that, every second that passes, even the hard ones, will be full of the richness of the glory of God. We are still at one with our purpose.

I was going through a very difficult situation. I didn't feel I deserved the pain, it wasn't my fault, someone else started it, and I was taking all the heat. I went to a friend's house for a long cup of tea and some encouragement. I wanted to tell someone how unfair everything was. I wanted to hear "You don't deserve this."

But the friend I went to see is a truth talker. She believes saying the hard things is better than saying the easy things. She turned the tables on me. "Look at you," she said. "You're sitting there playing in a pile of poo-poo. You're absolutely sitting in filth. And not only are you just sitting there, you're taking the dung and rubbing it all over your body and face, saying 'Look at me! Look at me!' to anyone who will listen. Come on now, you're better than that. It takes the bigger, more courageous person to look at everything that has gone wrong and, instead of turning to self-pity, look at how you can turn the negative into a positive. That's what you should be doing."

It was a wake-up call. I wanted everyone to feel bad for me. I wanted to feel bad for myself, but God doesn't call us to be seekers of self-pity. He tells us to be thankful in all circumstances—even those that are difficult and inexplicably painful. "Be joyful always; pray continually; give thanks in all circumstances, for this is God's will for you in Christ Jesus" (1 Thess. 5:16–18).

When I took my friend's advice, everything changed. I left my pity party and started recounting all the things for which I was thankful, and immediately I felt empowered. Thankfulness empowers. For when you are able to see purpose and possibilities even in the midst of turmoil, you tap into energy you didn't know you had.

While it's obviously contrary to our human nature to be thankful in pain, it is the most productive, healthy response we can have. Anger and self-pity only fuel self-hurt and waste time that we could be spending in God's plenty. To make the most of our God-given time, we must flip the coin on every unfortunate situation. We have to see the positive in the negative. We have to trust that His plan is greater than our plan. Even if we can't understand His goal, we have to remain faithful and give thanks.

To make the most of our 86400, we have to understand that the bitter helps us taste the sweet, that distance does make the heart grow fonder, and that strength is molded through pain. When a runner starts training, he cannot go very far. After training for months, he is ready for his marathon. He can compete. All of our circumstances, including the painful ones, truly do prepare us for our future.

A famous gospel song, "He's Preparing Me," reminds me that we should not lose sight of the need to be thankful in difficult times because God is preparing us for something greater. In order to prepare you, he has to bring you through something. When we operate with a thankful spirit, our vision remains fixed on the possibilities and opportunities made available to us even by unfortunate circumstances. Each 86400 affords an opportunity for God to prepare you to live your purpose!

86400 Adviser: David Brokaw—Thankfulness

David Brokaw learned early in life to see the blessings in a difficult situation that would cripple many people emotionally and spiritually. Today, Brokaw is one of the most successful dealmakers in the entertainment industry, whose sphere of influence extends far beyond Hollywood, but he grew up with a mother who was manic-depressive with "severe flip sides." Instead of being resentful or bitter about it, he was able to see humor in the situation and to see how it made him a strong, independent person.

"When I was growing up, one of the hardest things was my relationship with my mom," he said. "I love her dearly, but she suffers from mental illness. She's bipolar, manic-depressive—very high highs that often caused her to do funny and crazy things."

His mother had to enter hospitals several times for treatment with electroshock therapy during his childhood. Eventually, his parents broke up and he and his twin brother, Sandy, were raised by their father, Norman, chairman of the legendary William Morris Agency. "Our dad had to become a father and a mother, so my brother and I became very independent from a young age, and we took a keen interest in human behavior," Brokaw said. Their lives had to go on regardless, but their mother's troubles continued.

"I remember when my parents got divorced, she suddenly began handling her finances," he recalled. "One time, she was in a manic mood, and she ended up trading in the Mustang for a green Corvette. She got in the car and immediately got into an accident. She took a cab home but didn't have any money to pay the driver, so she gave him a TV."

When these things happened, he said, "It was funny to a degree. We could all tell our friends, 'You won't believe what my mom did last night,' but it was also difficult to watch." Given the circumstances, it would have been easy for him to wallow in self-pity, shame, or sadness, but he developed a brighter outlook. "I realized early on feeling sorry for myself wouldn't get me anywhere," he said. "While the experiences with my mom were difficult, they taught me to move on, to move past the heartache, and focus on the new possibilities of tomorrow. So in an odd way, I'm thankful for them." Thankful? It takes effort to see the blessing in such a situation, but he doesn't find his attitude unusual. "We were very blessed, because we had balance," he said. "Father has ethics and integrity, and a reverence for people in the business. Doing well, being effective, dressing well. We had a strong father present who taught us that it's one thing to make a mistake, but don't make it twice." He said parenting "was a big thing" for his father, who set a very high standard for his sons to follow.

"There are certain things that my father wanted for us," he added. "He had an idea of what he felt we should have and what we should do. I'm grateful for the strong love and bond with him, and so thankful that he pointed us in this direction. I'm thankful for his humble approach that he taught us: Get in and start doing something, build it and let it lead to something."

Transforming unique visions and compelling possibilities into dynamic, concrete, extraordinary reality is in David Brokaw's blood. His family has more than 120 years' experience in the entertainment industry, stretching back to czarist Russia. Brokaw's great-uncle, Johnny Hyde, was the man who discovered Marilyn Monroe.

David Brokaw, who runs the Brokaw Company with his brother, has made a career of bringing together ideas and opportunities, visions and realities. He is fully living his purpose. A mutual friend who thought we had similar sensibilities and could work on some projects together introduced us years ago. He was someone I wanted to know because of his openness and knowledge.

His company's list of clients reads like a who's who of entertainment and political change agents, including Loretta Lynn and Bill Cosby, among many others. Through marketing, promotion, public relations, feature films, television series, music projects, books, and other media, Brokaw successfully presents his clients to a worldwide audience. The company boasts that when *The Cosby Show, Roseanne,* and *A Different World* were the top three TV sitcoms, it handled the public relations for all three. Brokaw also has won numerous awards for his work bringing Cosby's *Little Bill,* a children's book that promotes positive values, to Nickelodeon. In spite of or because of his success, he continues to make thankfulness a habit. "Being thankful is the day," he said. "It shapes it, informs it. Without thankfulness, my day wouldn't be the same thing."

Living in a constant state of gratefulness opens the door to more opportunities that align him with his purpose. "When I get up in the morning I gaze at my garden," he said. "It's always blooming. I'm thankful for walking out the door and having a long driveway to walk down and pick up the *New York Times* and *LA Times*. I wonder what articles they contain today that will inspire me. Just thinking about thankfulness makes me in awe. It's humbling."

Consciously thanking others is another way he makes each day more effective and productive. "I used to tell the people working for me to call here or there, do this or that, and I noticed that some of them were moody and grumpy," he recalled. "I then started asking 'Could you please?' and saying 'Thank you' afterward, showing them that I was thankful for what they were doing. Immediately, there was a change in the climate of my office. Being thankful changes your environment in a positive way."

The biggest challenge he faces in getting the most out of his 86400, he said, "is to stay focused and to not get distracted.

"There are many ways to get distracted—Internet, phone calls, 'I wonder what so-and-so is doing?'" he added.

Brokaw stays on task by preparing the night before to have a purposeful day. Remaining purposeful "is a big thing that is comprised of a lot of little things," he said. "I have little things that I do and use as connective tissue; all the little things that I do allow me to do something big," Brokaw continued. "And change comes. I think about stuff I can do that will lead to big things. It's the single best way to maximize your time."

Thinking about how to make the most of his 86400, he said, brings to mind a Beatles song, "Nowhere Man," that says, "He's a real nowhere man/sitting in his nowhere land....Doesn't have a point of view...Isn't he a bit like you and me?"

"The simple answer is: You can't go blindly about your life," Brokaw said. "You have to be conscious of your time and what you are doing with it. If someone is going blindly from one thing to the next, they're lost, and lost people get nowhere."

Your Next 600 Seconds

Devote your next 600 seconds to thanking God for at least one person or thing that makes your life better than it would be without that individual or object. Consider all the things, material and immaterial, for which you should be thankful. Have you been through a difficult time but learned from it? Thank God for preparing you for the better times. Compose a prayer of thanksgiving that you could use every day.

Seconds for the Spirit

> *"Enter into his gates with thanksgiving, and into his courts with praise: be thankful unto him, and bless his name" (Ps. 100:4).*

THE FUTURE WE SEEK

—————

Future is a small word that has huge meaning. It encompasses the next moment, tomorrow, and every coming year. It's the script that hasn't been written and the events that have yet to be seen. The future is everything we have before us.

Right now, you're likely sitting down reading this book, and, since this is the beginning of a new section, five minutes from now you'll probably be doing the same thing, But five minutes from now doesn't have to be what you expect. You could set down this book and decide to treat yourself to a long, hot bath. You could go to the kitchen and try a new recipe. You could head to the garage and finally really try to fix the engine on that old car. While what you do in the next five minutes might not seem of paramount importance to you right now, every second we have is an ingredient that creates the second that comes next. The possibilities for your next 86400, while perhaps not infinite, are numerous. It's up to you to do what you want with them.

The future we seek is tied to how we perceive our purpose. It is that brighter tomorrow for which we all strive. That tomorrow you envision may include educational accomplishments, marriage and a family, a promotion at the job, or a thriving entrepreneurial venture. We all harbor images of a tomorrow, a not yet, a coming kingdom that ignites and excites us. That excitement about your vision allows you to enter into your purpose. The more crystal clear you can envision your future, the more purpose-filled your actions will be. The future we seek is critical in staying married to your purpose and making the most of your 86400.

In these next chapters, we're going to delve into personal characteristics that play a major role in the future we seek. Moment by moment, we are building the coming present.

Regardless of our political persuasion, we recognize that something profound happened when the United States elected its first African American president. A man from a race that had been enslaved was being sworn in as the leader of the country.

The conditions that allowed Obama to become president were made possible by the sacrifices and commitment of several generations of civil rights activists, dating from before Emancipation. Those who marched in the 1960s were preceded by those who fought for freedom even while enslaved. The future became possible because of the visionaries of the past—people who believed in a compelling future, a brighter tomorrow, and used their present actions for good yet to be seen. Those bound in slavery probably would rejoice to see who sits in the Oval Office today, for they must have believed that such was possible. Their energies were directed toward what they believed. Such achievements as the election of an African American president can only occur when they are first kernels of hope for a better future.

Songs of freedom have always pointed to the "not yet" or the kingdom coming. The classic gospel hymn "Hold On" is an example. With lyrics adjusted to speak to a better tomorrow, it became one of the anthems during the 1960s, shouting the chorus for all to hear: "I know the one thing we did right was the day we started to fight; keep your eyes on the prize. Hold on. Hold on."

Vision of a positive future is critical to making each day a testament to your purpose. It serves as your action's fuel, giving you the energy and inspiration to do more and be more with each precious 86400.

These next chapters are here to equip you with belief and clarity about your future. We can be motivated about the future or misled if we insist on the future we want rather than God's will.

"I do not pray for success. I ask for faithfulness," said Blessed Teresa of Calcutta, or Mother Teresa, the Roman Catholic missionary who died in 1997 (quoted from www .thinkexist.com), and that is my prayer for you. As you spend time looking deeper into the qualities of patience and faithfulness, I hope you learn the desires of your heart and take advantage of your possibilities. Be guided by the Kingdom of God rather than the Kingdom of Self and seek a future more bountiful and rewarding than you could ever dream.

7

Patience:
A Work in Progress

*The two most powerful warriors are
patience and time.*
—Lev Nikolayevich Tolstoy

One afternoon I went to the State Inspection Depot to get
my car inspected. Normally when I know I might have a
lengthy wait somewhere, I bring a book to read, but I'd
rushed out of the house and left my book. I arrived and
found an especially long line, with no magazines or news-
papers in sight. The place was filled with people staring into
space or toying with their cell phones. The wait was a test of
my patience. To pass the time I walked to the nearby guitar store. I've always been fascinated by guitars and wanted
to learn to play one. The extremely nice salesman sold me
an acoustic guitar, a case, and guitar lessons on Wednesday
afternoons at 4 p.m. and piano lessons at 5 p.m. By the way,
I did not have a piano. I returned to the inspection depot,
picked up my car, and off I went. (I had to put the top down
on my two-seater car because the guitar barely fit.) While

driving home, I told my friend Elinor all about the guitar, the music lessons, and the piano hunt I was on. "Funny you should mention that," she said. "My neighbor has a piano for sale." I rushed over, looked at it, and bought it on the spot.

Yes, I am somewhat impulsive. I did not think through any of my moves. Elinor reminded me that I had no time for music lessons with my current schedule. My schedule was very busy, filled with traveling, speaking engagements, and other commitments. She suggested I put off the lessons until my schedule slowed a bit. I declined because I was intent on learning immediately. Waiting was not an option.

For two Wednesdays straight, I rearranged meetings and other obligations so that I could go to piano and guitar lessons. My teachers were patient with me, even though I found no time to practice during the week and was just plain musically challenged! Those Wednesday lessons pulled me away from obligations. I became frustrated and cranky around Monday of each week because I knew I had to juggle to make those lessons.

A reasonable person would have taken one music lesson at a time. A patient person would have waited for a more opportune time to schedule the lessons, but that person was not me. My guitar sits in my den this very moment, a great conversation piece. The piano was not so lucky. It is hidden away in storage.

The entire experience left me frustrated. I still wonder if I have the capacity to learn to play guitar and piano. I needed a good dose of patience. Had I the patience to create a winnable and workable situation, I might be jamming lead guitar with my church choir right now.

The good news is that I learned that I don't need to do

everything right now. I have put what I learned from my guitar and piano lessons to good use.

I love all kinds of music, from R&B to country, but my all-time favorite is zydeco, a form of folk music that evolved in southwest Louisiana in the early nineteenth century from Creole music. I itch to start a zydeco band. I can see myself playing the washboard or the spoons. When I'm at home in Louisiana, I look for a zydeco dance and will often go up to the bandleader and ask if I can sit in to play the washboard. I recently played with a band at the church bazaar in Mallet, Louisiana. But here's the moral of my story: If I had become enamored with playing in a zydeco band years ago, I would have already bought a washboard and an accordion and be assembling a band by now. I've not given up on that dream, but I know that trying to do that right now would take me away from my purpose. For now, I'm still able to enjoy attending zydeco dances and playing in the band on occasion.

Learning to Slow Roast

Dreams of the future are so engrossing that we want them in our grasp no sooner than yesterday, but we are forever passengers of the present, the constantly forward-moving "right now." Without patience, nothing of substance will ever get accomplished. Patience is a state of endurance— persevering in the face of delay. When you live in the present and work for a future reality, delay is the name of the game. Without endurance through seconds, minutes, hours, days, months, and even years of delay, our purposed-laden dreams will never come to fruition, but with patience, we open ourselves up to blessings untold.

Look at the present-day world compared to the past, even a mere fifty years ago, and highlight our progress. Technology over the past few decades has sped forward. Every day there is something newer, quicker, and more intelligent. We can fly across the country in five hours. We can make an instant cup of coffee. We can store thousands of books on a handheld device. We are immediate-gratification connoisseurs, blessed with the best "right now" has to offer. We have misplaced patience. In the present day, it's so easy to be caught up. We can practically do what we want when we want. As a result, we feel patience isn't necessary. In the past, the pace of life didn't seem slow. People didn't methodically drum their fingers on the counter while waiting five minutes for their to-go order. People understood and expected that good things come to those who wait. They didn't believe in overnight answers and immediate satisfaction; they believed in the quality of time well spent.

When we evaluate how we can make the best use of our time and focus our energy to move forward with purpose, we don't often think that the answer is slowing down, or even taking a nap, as Reverend Cleage prescribed (see Chapter 4, "Balance: An Act of Love"). Instead of pausing, reflecting, and being intentional, we grab a bag of quick fixes. We make immediate, and occasionally thoughtless, decisions when we need to take a step back and be patient.

Picture this: You are on the road driving. You know where you want to go, but you're not entirely sure how to get there. You have a GPS in your bag stowed in your trunk, and it would certainly give you the lay of the land. Yet you also know that stopping, fishing it out, and setting it up would take time—and you're in a hurry to get to your goal. If you found yourself in this situation, would you (A) pull over, get out the GPS, and figure out the best route? Or would you (B) keep on driving and figure that making a few wrong turns would be quicker than asking for directions?

If you pick A, it will certainly take time. You will have to pull over, put on your hazard lights, and watch cars whip around you while you dig out the GPS. Still, you will, in all likelihood, reach your destination. If you pick B, while you will certainly get to keep driving, you don't have the guarantees of knowing where you are or the best routes to get where you want to go. What if—disastrously—you took a wrong, dangerous turn? Or you became confused in a roundabout? You would waste far too many valuable seconds going round and round the same circle.

You don't measure an effective life by how much you do and how quickly you do it. You measure it by the value of your experiences and your journey to your true goal. If you have the patience to figure out what you want to do, you will be far more likely to accomplish what you want. With patience, you will be able to take a deep breath, create a game plan with a clear head, and sincerely enjoy the process of achieving your desires.

Aged wine is valued. Thanksgiving turkey soaks in its marinade. Relationships develop over the course of months and years. The ability to speak another language, sew a quilt, play a guitar—those are all skills that develop over time.

I challenge you to take a step back in time and see the value of a slow roast. So much can happen if you allow yourself time so that you can become more discerning, intentional, effective.

PATIENCE

I met Federico Compean III when he spoke passionately about the state of Rotary International, a service organization of 1.2 million members and 33,000 clubs worldwide, at my River Oaks Rotary Club meeting. He was visiting from Monterrey, Mexico, where he is president of a company founded by his father that processes and exports Mexican spices, herbs, and other organic ingredients. Through fellow Rotarians, I was able to arrange an interview with him about the value of patience before he left for Mexico.

Federico Compean III
Rotary International coordinator and president of Compean International.

Patience is a virtue. It means to let yourself wait or spend enough time for things to have a better outcome. It is something you are not born with. It develops through time. The older you get, the more you see the value of patience. When you are fifteen, you want everything done yesterday. Not everything should be done yesterday. It is like cooking a meal. A sandwich is fast. Paella is very slow. Two different meals. Paella is much better than a sandwich, but it takes much longer. You have to put patience into it.

Raising your children, you can spank them, or you can have patience and teach them what they really should be doing. Patience is something that not everybody has, but it is something that everybody should have. If you are patient, enough things will come around. Things will come your way. You have a saying in the United States, "Good things shall come to those that wait." That's patience.

Everybody would like to have everything done immediately, or five minutes before. If you think about it, most things in your life that are worthwhile, patience has a big role in it. To get a husband or wife takes time and patience. You don't go out to the store and buy one. It takes patience because you have to develop a relationship, and that happens over time. If you want to raise a family, it takes a lot of patience. To begin with, it takes nine months for the child to get here. I have three kids and six grandkids. None of them was born with patience. No matter which way you slice it, patience has to come with time. As you get older, you find a great value in being patient.

There is a lot of stress in your life—why add anxiousness to it? We had Hurricane Alex in late June 2010, and it hit Monterrey. It destroyed Monterrey, and it took away my whole building and business. My computers, my office, raw materials, my machinery—everything was washed away. If I get anxious, I will not solve the problem. Not only will I not solve it, but I will make it even worse. My thinking will be obstructed by my actions. If I get mad, my thinking will not be clear. If I get desperate, my thinking will not be clear. In situations like this, what you need the most is a very clear and stable mind, and that is called patience. Let time do the talking and the helping. There is another saying, "The world was not made in one day."

With patience, my mind is stable and clear. A kid is very unstable. He wants to do everything. He wants to play, jump in a tree, eat, and watch TV all at the same time. You and I know that you cannot do that. So what you have to do is be patient. If I'm swimming, I cannot be watching TV. If you want to watch TV, stop swimming and go and watch TV, and vice versa.

Knowing how to distribute my time is what has helped me to be more productive and be a better manager of time—of when to wait and when to go. Things will be easier to perform if you give them more time.

The most valuable thing that any human being has is not your family, not your country, not your wealth—it is your time. If we did not have time, we would be six feet under, and if you are six feet under, your family, your country, your health, your wealth have no significance. We should be conscious of our 86400 because it is the most valuable thing we have. It is thanks to your time that you can do your job, your work. It is thanks to your time that you take a vacation. It is because of your time that you go and have a nice dinner tonight. It is because of your time that you have your husband, your children, or whatever the case may be. Because of your time, you can have a business, be productive, and generate wealth, not only for you but also for those who surround you.

It is a crime to steal time from other people because you are stealing the most valuable thing anybody has. Being punctual is something that should be rewarded. The other day I had a discussion with my dad and he said, "Freddy, but you are very punctual." I said, "Dad, there is no such thing as 'very punctual.' Either you are punctual or you are not." It is like when you are pregnant. You are not "very pregnant." You are or you are not.

What would you say if I stole my neighbors' daughter? I'd be in jail. Their daughter is not the most valuable thing they have. The most valuable thing is time. People steal time from people all the time, and it is as if most people don't care. People take it for granted. You take for granted the air we breathe. Go into a smoky situation and you will see how valuable it is. I'm at work before everyone and I leave after everyone, but if people are to be at work at 8 a.m., I expect them there at 8 a.m. I expect them to leave at 5 p.m., not 5:15 p.m., because if they cannot do their work from 8 to 5, one of two things is happening: One, you are giving them too much work, which is not fair, or, two, they are not doing it efficiently, which is not fair. Do 100 percent of your work and do it from 8 to 5.

There are 86400 seconds in a day, and this is not like a cellular phone where you can roll over your minutes. You use them and that's it. You don't get to roll them over to the next 86400. The next day you get the same number. With that being so and knowing that it is that way, we should value that 86400 so much more and make use of them very carefully. Although you get the same number each day, you are only getting so many days or 86400s more, because eventually we will die. Yesterday I was 86400 seconds richer than I am today. Tomorrow, I will be 86400 seconds poorer than I am today. Let's use those very, very carefully.

Now this does not mean that you have to work and work and work, or clean and clean. There should be time for everything. There should be time for work, or else you will not eat. There should be time for family, because they are very, very important. My family is most beneficial to me. They have backed me up in good times and bad, in my good decisions and in my bad decisions. There also should be time for food, cleaning, and TV, time for yourself. Set aside time for just doing nothing. It is like sleeping. Recharge yourself.

We are far more conscious of energy than we were ten years ago: "Go green!" and conserve this and that. We are making ourselves aware of it. The same thing has to be done with time and purpose. Put it on the radar.

My purpose or the only reason that I am here in this life is to be happy. How do I accomplish me being happy when there are so many things around us that are trying to destroy that? First of all, happiness is not a total concept. You are not happy 100 percent of the time. The thing is to have more happy moments than unhappy moments. How are you going to do that? Once you know that you are not going to be happy 100 percent of the time, it is very simple. The only way I can be happy is if I have my little circles around me happy. I wake up very happy, but if I came in very late and very drunk last night, my wife is not going to be very happy. If I wake up very happy, but she is unhappy, that will make me unhappy, too. If my wife and I are very happy, but one of our grandkids is in the hospital, then we are unhappy, because that circle of mine is unhappy. Then you grow that to your friends, your business. You can't be happy 100 percent of the time. You will have unhappy moments in order to value those happy moments.

My destiny is service, but I serve because I have to be happy. So in order to be happy, I have to work a lot in or around my circles for my people to be happy. I do my best to have them happy as much as possible.

I have been with Rotary for forty years. My grandfather was a Rotarian. My dad is a Rotarian. So I have always been involved with Rotary. I like to serve. Maybe it is selfish, because I get the biggest joy out of it. Rotary lets me serve in a very well-organized manner. It lets me serve with very nice people and on an international level. My father and grandfather were district governors, and I was a district governor. The funny thing is that I was a district governor before my dad was. Rotary is in my blood.

I travel a lot with Rotary and Rotary Foundation, talking and giving seminars, looking at projects. Very frequently I go into villages to help people have drinkable water. The smile of a little kid who had a glass of water, you cannot buy that, you cannot trade it. You have to live it. We have a hearing-aid program through my Rotary in Monterrey. The smile of that little kid who hears her mother's voice for the first time—you cannot buy that, but that makes me happy that she is happy.

Many people serve because they think that is the way to Heaven. That is fine. Many serve because that is the way to pay for their misbehaving or sins. People serve because it is very gratifying to serve. That is why it is selfish. The giver is the one who is getting the best part of the deal.

Money is not everything. It is just the means. Most people and most problems that we have in our world are related to wealth. Wealth is something you need, but it is not always counted in dollars and cents. Wealth is when you have a lot of friends, good health, and liberty. If people would concentrate more on the value of things that are wealth and less on the money aspects of that wealth, they not only will live longer but also be happier and more content with what they have.

I'm not saying go sit on the sofa and watch TV all day. You have to work, but don't go to the other extreme—all work. We are struggling twenty-four hours a day. When we sleep, we are sweating because our business did not go well and thinking, *How am I going to do it?* I say do as much as you can, the best way you can, but there is just so much you can do. Know your limits. When you reach a limit, sometimes things open up more possibilities, so you raise your limits, your limit goes up. Keep on going up the ladder, but don't run up the ladder, because you will fall. Be patient, one step at a time. Don't jump three steps.

Be aware that you can always do things better. Fight. A lot of people are easily discouraged; they give up quickly. If they fall down, they don't want to stand up again. They are demoralized, and maybe patience has something to do with it. If they would be patient, maybe they would say, "Well, I did not do it this time; I'll get up and try it again." Never go back. A Spanish saying says, "Don't take steps back, not even to get momentum going—never back, always forward."

Don't Let the Anger Out of the Bag

Patience helps us make informed, wise decisions. It helps us avoid wasting our time by making certain that we are headed in the right direction. It gives us the space to weigh our options, listen to words of guidance, and make the best choice.

Patience is essential because of the unhealthy characteristics it keeps at bay. It helps us *respond*, rather than *react*. The twists and turns, toils and snares of life do not derail us from our purpose because patience helps us to keep our emotions under control.

Many good people, in a brief instant, have made a bad decision that radically changed the trajectory of their lives. Fear, anger, jealousy, lust, or other unrestrained emotions prevented them from slowing down and making a level-headed decision. Their souls, filled with regret, say, "If only I had a chance to do it over again." What they are saying is they wish they had deployed the powerful panacea of patience. Had they acted with patience, they would have reflected on their purpose, their goals, their dreams and aspirations and proceeded based on those rather than immediate gratification.

Life is full of difficult and painful situations. People do things that hurt us and make us angry (and we do the same to others). It is our choice how we respond. We can lash out and amplify the hurt, or we can take a step back, truly listen, take a deep breath, and then respond from a Godly place of understanding, patience, and mercy.

I've recently tried to adopt the twenty-four-hour policy. If I am tempted to lash out, I have to wait twenty-four hours. During that 86400, I get my feelings out by writing a letter. I say how the person hurt me and why it really got under my skin. After I get all of those feelings out on the table, I throw the letter away. I examine myself. Usually the person who hurt me apologizes because he realized he was quick with his tongue and didn't mean the things he said, or I realize that the person's words were hurtful because they were true. It is hard to hear how I am flawed, and my automatic reaction is to point the finger the other way. Now my twenty-four-hour policy gives me the time to understand that the other person wasn't in the wrong; it was me all along.

Could you imagine if everyone in the world were required to adopt the twenty-four-hour policy? How many more friendships would be intact? How many more marriages would be healthy? How many fewer car accidents would there be on the road? How much happier, in general, could your life be?

God understands the power of the tongue coupled with expedience. James 1:19–20 reads: "My dear brothers, take note of this: Everyone should be quick to listen, slow to speak and slow to become angry, for man's anger does not bring about the righteous life that God desires." Or James 3:5–6: "Likewise the tongue is a small part of the body, but it makes great boasts. Consider how a great forest is set on fire by a small spark. The tongue also is a fire, a world of evil among the parts of the body. It corrupts the whole person, sets the whole course of his life on fire, and is itself set on fire by hell."

If I lash out when others do, word bomb falls upon word bomb. We both are injured, perhaps even scarred. If I have the self-control and the patience to wait until I can respond with understanding, Christ's guiding light keeps me on the pure path of intention for my life.

Trial under Fire

Patience helps achieve your purpose, and patience helps you react wisely with intentional decisions. The simple truth is, patience is often elusive when it is most needed and when life is difficult. Sometimes you are thrown into very hard, unexpected situations and you can't see an end to them. For example, maybe you lost your job and don't know how you will find another one. Maybe you just went to the doctor and found out that the little lump that had been worrying you wasn't benign at all. For the next few months, you'll have to work hard and have endurance to try to beat the disease. How patient could you be waiting for a job or the next test results to show you are cancer free?

When life is hard, I want to move hard in the other direction. In my most human moments, I want to give up and go somewhere else. When I am experiencing trial under fire, I need to search for patience the most. For it is during those trying times that my resolve is tested. We have all been there when distress tries to prod our purpose from our heart's grasp. Psalms 40:1–3 says, "I waited patiently for the LORD; he turned to me and heard my cry. He lifted me out of the slimy pit, out of the mud and mire; he set my feet on a rock and gave me a firm place to stand. He put a new song in my mouth, a hymn of praise to our God. Many will see and fear and put their trust in the LORD."

As much as we want it to, life doesn't happen on our time. We can push and pull and force all we want, but typically when we tamper with the nature of things, we tamper with their potentially glorious outcomes. The best cheese is aged. Humans mature. It is in time that nature develops things for the benefit of those who endure.

The story of Job is one of the hardest stories to read in the Bible because it is a story of man's struggle and pain, of one who learns to endure the hardships of life. Most of us try to skip through it quickly, wanting to find the parts with singing angels again and God giving us the ability to move mountains. However, the struggle is just as essential. Learning to have patience in the valleys means we have to rely on our faith more than we do, and God blesses his children continually in their faithfulness and in their staying the course living out their purpose as God intended.

If you take the time to read all of Job, inevitably you'll come to the epilogue—the end of the struggle. There the story finishes, "The LORD blessed the latter part of Job's life more than the first.... After this, Job lived a hundred and forty years; he saw his children and their children to the fourth generation. And so he died, old and full of years" (Job 42:12; 16–17).

What an amazing story and what crucial words: "After this." So often when we are in the midst of our heartaches, we cannot see what has come before and certainly cannot see what will come after. It is sitting in a deep dark pit with walls all around us. Always, there is an "after this." Something can be gleaned from our patience.

Patience gives us all the time we need to become the people God intends for us to be. In our bouts of difficulty and trial, we should run to His understanding and follow His command: "Be still and know that I am God" (Ps. 46:10).

86400 Adviser: Ricky Anderson—Patience

As a lawyer, Ricky Anderson has learned that patience is often the difference between winning or losing and that sometimes the best use of his 86400 is to do nothing. When he makes a move, the wait pays off, allowing him to proceed with purpose.

"As a legal counselor, patience is essential," he said. "We have to give counsel and that counsel has to be meaningful, which requires thoughtfulness and demands patience. Quickly, you learn to be a patient listener and a patient communicator. While this might seem to take up more of my 86400 to begin with, it saves so much time in the long run. Taking the time and having the patience to hear the whole story, explain things thoroughly, and do things right—there might not be anything as effective in managing your time and purpose."

Anderson is managing partner of the Houston, Texas, law firm of Anderson & Smith P.C., where he develops deals for network television, movies, feature films, pay-per-view, and HBO. He represents numerous celebrities, including actor Isaiah Washington and gospel artist Yolanda Adams, as well as the actor/comedians Steve Harvey and Mo'Nique. He is also the chairman and chief executive officer of the Black Broadcasting Network, Inc., and majority shareholder in Big City Enterprises, producing national concerts such as the *Kings of Comedy.*

Ricky is a dear friend of mine, and I have worked with him on numerous projects over the past fifteen years, learning from his patient example. Along the way I have found that he is well respected for his work ethic, honesty, and ability to get things done with integrity, efficiency, and purpose.

"I've sat through a number of tireless negotiations on a deal that lasts for months and months because people can't agree," he said. "Sometimes it might feel like a waste of time, but you have to remain professional and realize that this agreement is a huge marker for a number of people. If at the end of the months of negotiations, they can't agree to terms, it can be frustrating because it feels like there was all that disagreement and heartache for no benefit. But the patience to endure it helps you see both sides more clearly."

In such cases, Anderson said, you have to remember that there are three sides to every story: the client's, the opposition's, and the truth. "You have to have the ability to discern the difference between them because the facts won't change," he said. "That's where you have to have the patience and wherewithal to analyze and articulate your position in a positive capacity. The key to success is clear, transparent communication, and, again, that requires patience.

"Static gets avoided with patience," he said. When he has worked for months on a deal that does not close because the parties cannot come to terms, it is particularly frustrating. "You've got to remain professional with whomever," he noted. "It may be one of the major TV networks or a production house. Accepting the fact that you disagree and you are unable to close the deal takes patience, and at the end of the day you move on.

"For professional success as an attorney, you always have to have patience with your opposition, because it is a combative relationship by nature," he added. "By definition, you are opposing counsel, and from the beginning, you have to have that professional courtesy."

The same kind of patience is equally important in everyday life, he said. "Patience is absolutely key from an emotional perspective. So often, people want to react immediately to situations. They want to give their gut reactions. As a legal counselor, I see this all the time, but patience allows you not to react emotionally. It allows you to step back and view a situation with a clear mind. Taking time, you hear what the person is saying, you have to digest it, analyze it, react to it, and then respond."

Anderson finds great motivation in creating an empowered future. His forward thinking makes him acutely aware of the value of each 86400 and the need to stay focused on his life's mission and purpose. "Self-motivation has been beneficial to my success—the ability to be driven within, an internal drive that I'm able to tap into," he said. "My drive to act, to move, to do, and to help is based on my desire to contribute to my family, my profession, and society as a whole."

Routinely waking up at 4 a.m., he fits in a workout before tackling conference calls and e-mails en route to his office for meetings, teleconferences, negotiations, and travel—ever mindful of using each second well. "It is important to be conscious of your 86400 because time is invaluable," he said. "Time is priceless. Life is based on time. You will run out of it sooner or later."

Again, he says, the key is patience. "Patience, with respect to your day, allows you to take a deep breath," Anderson explains. "You have to be conscious of how you manage and allocate your time." Each of us has to recognize that our day, our 86400, is priceless and irreplaceable. It is a commodity to be valued. Once those seconds are exhausted, they are gone.

Those of us who are not so sure-footed must first evaluate where we are and, based on that evaluation, take steps to move forward. Anderson said that might require reaching out to others for help, obtaining more education, or developing new habits to reach the place where we ultimately want to be.

Even amid his professional obligations and the pressures, he reserves time for God and family. "Everybody has a life," he adds. "I'm a husband, father, brother, son, and more, with lots of responsibility, so I have to be conscious and careful of how I allocate my time. With me, God is first, then family, and my profession. You have to be a good Christian and a good person, and that leads to being a good professional, and ultimately that leads to success."

Your Next 600 Seconds

Devote your next 600 seconds to considering how you could be more patient. Think back to a time when you might have made a life-changing decision without being as patient as you should have been and suffered the consequences or hurt someone else because of your haste. Try to recall a time when you witnessed the power of patience. Reflect on how patience could help you maximize your 86400, reach your goals, and live your purpose.

Seconds for the Spirit

> *"We do not want you to become lazy, but to imitate those who through faith and patience inherit what has been promised"* (Heb. 6:12).

8

Faithfulness:
Perseverance in Purpose

Listen to the mustn'ts, child. Listen to the don'ts.
Listen to the shouldn'ts, the impossibles, the won'ts.
Listen to the never haves, then listen close to me—
Anything can happen, child. Anything can be.
—Shel Silverstein

My mother, grandmother, father, and others serenaded me with an ongoing chorus of directives to stay faithful. "Have faith in God and His plan for you," they would say with conviction, no matter what the circumstance. I believed them then, and I believe them now. What really gave me the ability to trust their words, however, were their actions.

They, particularly my mother, had faith in me. As I have gotten older and more reflective, I am amazed that my mother still believes in me. Her faith in me strengthened my faith in myself. She never stops mothering, guiding, encouraging.

I "can do all things through Christ" who strengthens me, as the Scripture says in Philippians 4:13, because my mother continuously told me I could.

Silverstein was the author of such books as *The Giving Tree, Where the Sidewalk Ends, A Light in the Attic*, and *Falling Up*. He delighted children and made them curious. With Shel Silverstein, anything could happen.

Like the Silverstein quote about listening to the "mustn'ts," many of us, beginning in our infancy, have been told the things we cannot do, the people we cannot be. Silverstein was telling children such concepts of ordinariness weren't true.

Silverstein's words are deeply in tune with the Bible. God has not called us to lives of complacency or ordinariness. He has called us to be a part of His kingdom—an extraordinary, miraculous, uncommon life. To internalize Silverstein's words requires faithfulness, supreme confidence in the "not yet." Faithfulness is displaying so much confidence in the "not yet" reality, the "not yet" achieved goal, or the "not yet" life desired that you act as if it already is. Faithfulness offers us powerful support as we seek to live our lives with intention and purpose. To me, *faith* implies belief in something, but *faithfulness* implies a continuing process of being conscientious and steadfast in pursuing our purpose. Faithfulness inspires us to persevere and continue working toward our not-yet-achieved reality in spite of doubts and fatigue. Faithfulness is a prerequisite for making the most of your 86400.

Silverstein's promise that we can be extraordinary becomes a reality when we take the risk of stepping out on faith and believing that we can be more, do more, and achieve more than the world tells us we can. This faithfulness empowers our 86400.

When you live in faithfulness, you become more conscious of how you spend your time. You not only plan better and in more detail, you operate better. Your actions are not empty, hollow, or self-destructive. Studies have found that even though savage inequalities still exist in education depending on a child's zip code and his or her parents' financial statement, the single greatest determinant for a child's educational success is expectation. If a student has a teacher, parents, community, or all of the above who have faith in that child's ability, that child will likely excel regardless of socioeconomic status, gender, race, or attending a resource-poor school. Those who study such matters say that the faith others have in a student is internalized to the point that the child expects educational excellence. That child's 86400 is entirely different from the 86400 of the child labeled "unteachable." Psychologists, sociologists, and educators are finding that the only difference between the genius and the soon-to-be dropout is the level of faithfulness in them and around them. The child operating with faith in his or her successful future is faithful to the task. That child studies longer, reads more than required, takes advantage of tutoring sessions, and seeks out enrichment opportunities. The difference is not genetics or economics, it's faithfulness.

Educator Jaime Escalante, the high-school math teacher who inspired the 1988 movie *Stand and Deliver*, proved this. Escalante had so much faith in his predominantly poor and Latino students, even though they had been declared uneducable, they began to have faith in themselves and each other. The rest, as they say, is history. Escalante's students were faithful to the work, becoming so successful in his math classes that their grades went up in all their classes. Most graduated from high school and went on to college. They were no different from their peers in terms of economic status, family drama, and neighborhood challenges. The only difference between Escalante's students and the others was their faith in themselves and their faithfulness to the task of maximizing their potential.

This same dynamic is being played out in the national constellation of KIPP (Knowledge Is Power Program) schools. These schools work primarily with student populations that have historically been on the wrong side of the achievement gap, the term applied to the tendency of African American and Latino students to score far below peers in standard testing. The faith KIPP administrators, teachers, and parents have in their students is infectious and has created an achievement dynamic that many charter schools and traditional public schools are seeking to emulate.

KIPP schools operate under such simple directives as "Work hard and be nice." Theirs is not a blind faith, or a faith without actions. Rather, it is faith that promotes making the best use of one's 86400. It is faithfulness that promotes the best use of one's time. Teachers routinely stay later. Students regularly attend Saturday classes. Parents know they are required to be present and participate. Applying faithfulness, everybody steps up their game and maximizes their God-given 86400.

Faithfulness can empower you.

Nelson Mandela was fond of quoting author Marianne Williamson's classic, *A Return to Love*: "Our deepest fear is not that we are inadequate. Our deepest fear is that we are powerful beyond measure. It is our light, not our darkness that most frightens us. We ask ourselves, Who am I to be brilliant, gorgeous, talented, fabulous? Actually, who are you not to be? You are a child of God. Your playing small does not serve the world. There is nothing enlightened about shrinking so that other people won't feel insecure around you. We are all meant to shine, as children do. We were born to make manifest the glory of God that is within us. It's not just in some of us; it's in everyone. As we let our own light shine, we unconsciously give other people permission to do the same. As we are liberated from our own fear, our presence automatically liberates others."

Williamson, Mandela, and Silverstein understand the inordinate possibility of a faith-filled life. As followers of God, this possibility is exponentially greater.

Faith is difficult. Believing we are capable of leading extraordinary lives is challenging, if we have been told the opposite our entire lives. Understanding that God's plan is greater than our plan helps us reject other people's opinions and accept God's dominion over us. We have to hand Him our lives and say, with complete truth, "It's all Yours."

Walt Disney is widely quoted as having once said, "When you believe in a thing, believe in it all the way, implicitly and unquestionable." This is the key to Christianity.

FAITHFULNESS

Years ago, when I was an instructional supervisor, I frequently visited Jack Yates Senior High School in Houston, where Roland Martin, now a CNN contributor, attended. Martin's success continues to provide inspiration and hope to many of the school's students, and I have witnessed firsthand the positive influence that Martin's success has had on many other students in the Houston area. As a journalist and author, he is candid and meticulous, and faith plays a major part in his success at making the most of his God-given time.

Roland Martin
CNN contributor, commentator for TV One Cable Network, host of *Washington Watch with Roland Martin,* journalist and author.

There are some people who look at faith as a part of their life, and there are those like me who look at faith as the essence of their life. Here's an example of what I mean. Years ago, I was watching *Nightline* and the issue had to do with homosexuality. There were people on the panel from the faith world, people who were gay and lesbian, et cetera. Before Ted Koppel asked a question, he said, "Let's put the issue of faith away for a moment." I sat there and I said, "He just made a big mistake. Putting faith aside is part of the problem."

There are some who see faith through the prism of "I look at all things through my faith" and some that say "Well, I can put faith aside, so that I can focus on some other things." That to me is the big difference. For me faith is the essence of my life. I see all things through faith. I think faith is vitally important to your day, your seconds in each day. Faith helps to get you through the day. If you are not conscious of your 86400, you will allow it to get away from you and you're left asking yourself, What did I achieve? I really believe in maximizing every moment, all of my 86400. People always ask me, "How do you do all that you do? How do you write columns, host radio shows, television shows, give speeches, et cetera?" It is because I am fully aware of the time, my time, my 86400. I'm fully aware of what is in front of me and what I have to get accomplished.

I'm on the Tom Joyner morning show every day. I have a connecting line in my house. I wake up at 6 a.m. I've done the research, and I'm prepared, so I walk across to the living room and do my segment that starts at about 6:15 Central, for ten minutes. I might work out with my trainer at 6:30 a.m. or 7:30 a.m., then I come back and I get some work done. I might go back to sleep or take a nap. As the day progresses, I might get phone calls, e-mails that I have to handle. CNN may call and request me to go on the air. I might work on my column or any number of things, depending on where I am. I might have a speaking engagement out of town, so I might be on a plane right after the morning show. I have a whole lot of stuff packed in a day, but it ebbs and flows.

I utilize technology to be more efficient. A woman was upset because I used my BlackBerry in church. She said I should not type my sermon notes into my BlackBerry, because people will think I'm texting in church. Well, first of all, people should mind their own business. I type my sermon notes into my Black-Berry. Then I upload my sermon notes to my blog, my Facebook page, and some of the information to my Twitter account. That's 100,000 people I'm sharing the gospel with by the virtue of typing it into my BlackBerry as opposed to writing it down. That is being efficient with my time. By the time we are into the benediction, I'm blessing 100,000-plus people who may not have gone to church or who have missed it. I use technology to my advantage. My BlackBerry is the tool that helps me be successful. I get a number of things done via e-mail and texting.

A second tool that has helped me to be successful is I have honed and developed a concept taken from attorneys. That concept is having a billable-hour mentality. What that means is, my time is money. Time is valuable. The way I look at it is that I'm a 750-dollar-an-hour person. I value even an hour of doing nothing—that is, my time to think, to be creative. As you go about your 86400 ask yourself, Did I just give somebody two hours of my time when I could have been generating $1500 worth of income in those two hours?

It's about putting people on your schedule and not allowing people to dominate your schedule. That makes me more efficient and most effective. I'm in total command of the schedule at all times. I will tell folks what I can and cannot do. I'm very efficient. I take those things that are standard and locked in and build my schedule completely around that.

Faith is the essence of my life, and my faith inspires me to do a number of things. I've always used my various platforms to talk about faith. When I had my syndicated column, I wrote about various contemporary topics through the faith prism—whether it was a column dealing with a baseball player who made a decision not to play a particular game because it was a Jewish holiday or about the YWCA diminishing the Christian aspect of their name. When I ran www.blackamericaweb.com, Tom Joyner's site, there was no faith channel. I said, "There is no way you can have a Web site targeting black people and there's no faith channel." So I added that. I've always integrated my faith perspective in those lights.

I write books for the same reasons. The 50 perspectives that I talk about in my book *Listening to the Spirit Within: 50 Perspectives on Faith* are timeless. You can look at them as 50 distinct pieces. They don't have to go in any particular order. They can speak to you in many different ways.

My faith also provides me comfort. When you are in prayer, and you are taking something to God, asking for the proper direction for what it is that you are doing, then you have comfort in knowing full well that you can handle what is ahead of you. In difficult times, my faith helps me to look for discernment and ask God what his will is for me.

Discernment is vitally important. It is the most critical as far as I'm concerned. People make a genuine mistake all the time. That is, they will say, Hey! I hope this works out for the better. I hope this happens and that happens, as opposed to really asking themselves a very vital and important question and that is: Is this really God's intent for me? Is this God's purpose for what it is I'm trying to do? You have to ask yourself, Is this God's will?

I'm often asked, "How do you have such clarity?" We all have our own ideas of what it is that we want to do, want to achieve. We never really ask, Where does God want to use me? Where does God want me to flourish? My advice to people is to sit still and ask God. People are so afraid to sit still and allow God to speak to their minds and their hearts and soul—to gain the direction that they actually need. They mope around or talk to a friend. Do all this stuff, and God is sitting there and saying, "Hey! I'm trying to let you know right now."

I tell everybody that there is a process. I found that quiet place in my home that is my place of refuge. I don't care if you have kids or if you are married. You have to find that one place that is your "everybody off limits" place: "Unless this place is on fire or you need to go to the emergency room, don't disturb me." You can go to this place and cleanse, meditate, let God speak to you. When I go into a situation, I always ask God to speak to me, speak to my mind, remove me from the situations and allow his words to come forward.

Feel-Good Faith

Strong faith is valuable for our health. The power of a positive heartbeat is tied to our spiritual beliefs. When we pray and truly rest on our faith, our physical nature and bodily health increase. Your religious practices and beliefs are positively linked to the physiology of your brain, according to *How God Changes Your Brain: Breakthrough Findings from a Leading Neuroscientist*, by Andrew Newberg and Mark Robert Waldman (Ballantine, 2010). The authors, who are academics with the University of Pennsylvania's Center for Spirituality, argue that faith can alter everything about you—from your mind-set to your biology. This work suggests that faith and the spiritual practices associated with it can predispose you to live your purpose.

This is nothing new to Christian believers. Faith is what gets us through. It is our shot of adrenaline, second wind, encouragement, and our constant partner in intellectual pursuits, in sickness, and in any challenge.

In the Bible (Matt. 9:20–22; Mark 5:25–34; and Luke 8:43–47), a woman suffering from what is described in all three passages as "an issue of blood" is seeking the help of Jesus to provide her with a cure. This blood, in her time and culture, made her ritually "unclean." She was supposed to remove herself voluntarily from society so as not to rub up against another person, thereby making them ritually "unclean" as well. However, this woman wanted healing. When she heard that this great healer Jesus was coming her way, she threw social convention to the wind and pressed her way through the crowd to get to Jesus, if only to touch the hem of His garment, these Scriptures tell us.

Once she got near Jesus and grabbed the edge of His robe, Jesus felt power leave His body. The woman was healed instantly. Afraid she would be punished by Jesus' Disciples or any member of the crowd who had gathered, she stood there almost frozen (Mark 5:33 says, "trembling with fear") after Jesus asked the question: "Who touched me?" His Disciples were confused by the question as at that point quite a crowd had amassed and nearly everyone was rubbing up against each other. But the woman knew what Jesus was really asking and she admitted to being the one. She explained to Jesus her quest for healing and thanked him for healing her, but Jesus told her, "Your faith has made you whole" (Mark 5:34).

It is our faith that makes us whole. It binds up our insecurities, it suffocates our doubts, and it heals our heartbreaks. No wonder Newberg and Waldman found scientific proof that religious belief provided physical strength. Our faithfulness is the most certain way we can be totally well and focused on living a life of purpose and intention.

86400 Adviser: Daymond John—Faithfulness

Daymond John, chief executive officer of FUBU, the multimillion-dollar fashion empire and fashion innovator, is a walking example of the power of faithfulness.

When he conceived his business, he believed in his idea so much that he burned his material possessions and stepped out on faith—just as the Bible tells us Elisha did to follow the prophet Elijah (1 Kings 19:21).

"I took a second mortgage out on my home because I couldn't get a loan at the bank," Daymond said. "I went home, I took all my furniture, everything I owned, and I put it in my backyard, and I burned it. In place of everything, I set up sewing machines. For years, I slept next to those sewing machines. While I'm sure to outsiders it seemed crazy, I had faith I was doing the right thing."

The old furnishings had to go to make room in his house in Hollis, Queens, New York, to sew the clothes that he dreamed he could produce and mass-market after years of selling custom-made clothes one piece at a time. That was the tangible reason, but it was also an act of faith—faith in himself, in his idea, and in his ability to carry it out.

"In the beginning of any new project or idea, your own faith is essential because the world is full of people who try to talk you down and tell you about 'reality,'" he said. "Their words, no matter the intention, set you back, but if you have faith in yourself, you can move forward without the doubts and hesitations. You can be firmly rooted in your hopes and in your plans."

FUBU originally stood for Five Urban Brothers United, referring to him and the friends who helped him launch the company in 1992. It came to be known as For Us, By Us and that explanation of the acronym stuck. The initial dream was to create street-smart hats for the urban youth market. Today, the company makes casual wear, sportswear, suits, eyewear, belts, and shoes and has a diverse market.

Faith allowed Daymond John to proceed with unbridled perseverance, purpose, and a passion to redefine fashion and cater to a market of hip young people who were otherwise ignored. He quickly transformed a dream into an enterprise that has won numerous accolades. I initially met Daymond when a mutual friend introduced us, paving the way for me to pick Daymond's brain regarding a fashion concept I had.

"A lot of having a strong faith is equipping yourself with the knowledge," he said. "I don't react, I respond. I plan. I research. I know what I'm getting into and I know my abilities. Once you know all of the hard facts there are to gather, you have to have faith in the unknown." Mass production of clothing was new to him, but he went into it trusting that he knew what to do.

Searching for words to define faithfulness, he said, it "is so close to the concept of love—love in a sense of loving your life and what you do, having confidence in it.

"If you don't have faith, everything you touch will crumble," he said. "Consider this: If you're headed in a direction but don't have faith in that direction, you'll easily be swayed to change your course. If you don't have faith in yourself or in your self-worth, you will easily be convinced that who you are isn't good enough, but equipping yourself with faith is following a higher power and staying committed to what you know to be true. Faith is confidence of the heart."

To market his clothes, for instance, Daymond John said he was doing "product placement" long before many others were. "Instead of running commercials, I put the product on people in videos," he said. "I had faith in what I was doing and in the market and I let it sell itself. As we know now, it ended up working."

These days, Daymond John is a highly sought-after speaker on branding, business, and motivation who inspires diverse audiences with his story of sacrifice, hard work, perseverance, and faith.

"Once you set your mind to it, get after it," he tells people, "don't let the naysayers stand in your way. What if Edison listened to the ones who didn't have faith in him? They may have told him to make a bigger candle or a brighter one, instead of the lightbulb, or they may have told Ford to make a faster horse instead of a car. But they had faith in the same way I strive to have faith, and that belief keeps me productive because I'm moving forward, not standing still with my time."

Managing his 86400 well and living out his purpose requires goal setting, Daymond said. "Setting goals allows you to think things through and track progress," he said. "Set your goals. I set my goals every night and every morning. When you set goals, writing them down, you reaffirm what you want in life, in business, in everything. You will become what you think about. Goals offer clarity and direction."

Recording the goals also helps to establish timetables, he argues, because people tend "to overestimate what they can do in one year and they underestimate what they can accomplish in ten years."

Goals are an integral part of John's marathon workdays. He rattles off a precise schedule for each one of them: He rises at 8 a.m. after only three hours' sleep. First thing on the agenda, he said, is to read his goals. He usually has a long walk to the gym and an early workout. At the office, he puts in hours of meetings and calls. If he missed his workout, at three o'clock he multitasks, working out on his office tread-mill while handling calls to maximize his time. In the evening, his workday continues with dinner meetings, followed by research until midnight and brainstorming until 2 a.m.

Long after most people have gone to bed, it still isn't over. From 2 a.m. to 5 a.m., he goes out for the all-important fashion sourcing—to check out what people are wearing at a studio or club, or to meet a new artist. After he finally heads home, he checks his goals again before fitting in a little sleep.

The entrepreneur lives by the Confucian proverb "The man who moves a mountain does so one pebble at a time" as he continues to move his mountain, one second, one hour, one day at a time. "You have to manage your time wisely," he said. "Goal setting will help you do this. Parcel out your days. Work with intention, and keep the process and finish line in mind. If you say and pursue it, you will achieve it."

Your Next 600 Seconds

Devote your next 600 seconds to considering ways that you might be more faithful. Have there been times when you have not been so faithful to your purpose? Do you know why? Define faithfulness in your own words. Would you call yourself a faithful person? Why or why not? Consider how faithfulness can help you make the most of your God-given time and fulfill your purpose.

Seconds for the Spirit

"Press on toward the goal to win the prize for which God has called me heavenward in Christ Jesus" (Phil. 3:14).

THE LIFE WE'RE
INTENDED TO LEAD

———

God expects us to live lives of purpose. In Genesis, the Lord makes it clear that we are supposed to have dominion over His creation. We have been charged with the mission and purpose of assuming responsibility for the well-being of the planet and all its inhabitants. How your role in all that plays out is between you and God. The Lord gave you unique gifts and talents to carry out your purpose. Some African cultures believe the realm of dreams is more real than their daily-awakened lives. They are right. Our dreams of pushing past the monotonous, being more daring, giving graciously, reaching for the sky without inhibitions, reflect a more accurate picture of the life God intended for us to lead.

We were created with unlimited potential and capacity to be bold, innovative, life transforming, and world changers. Your mind, body, and spirit are telling you to reach for meaning, purpose, fulfillment, and joy. Gnawing inner pains are often messages from your true divine nature to unlock your higher, better, more spontaneous self. In the final two chapters, we will be taking a close look at two characteristics that help us embrace the life we're intended to lead:

generosity and courage. Both are distinct contributors to forward movement and future success. When we learn to give—of our heart, our hopes, our time, our goods, and our spirit—we will reach the pinnacle of God's purpose for our lives.

9

Generosity:
The Power of Giving

Do all the good you can,
By all the means you can,
In all the ways you can,
In all the places you can,
At all the times you can,
To all the people you can,
As long as ever you can.
—John Wesley

Years ago a complete stranger, AnneMarie Wallace, who is now a very dear friend, was most generous toward me. I was going about my very blessed life, doing my thing. I wasn't a bad person. I was raised in the church, went to a Catholic school, and possessed a good spiritual foundation. But as an adult I became self-absorbed and pushed God far in the background of my life.

One evening I decided to attend a Christmas party for the homeowners in my building. My intent was not to mix and mingle, just to get something to eat and sky out of there as soon as possible. I was about to make my exit when AnneMarie introduced herself and engaged me in a conversation. I forgot my mission and found this very soft-spoken platinum blonde a delight to talk with.

AnneMarie was extremely open about her faith, though not preachy at all. She was generous enough to open up her world to me. She invited me to 1st Corinthians 13 Church. She volunteered with a group of African American girls at the church and said it would be great if I would meet some of them.

I started hanging out with AnneMarie. I began to see things differently. Long talks with her and witnessing the life of service she lived made me examine what I was doing with the time God had given me. From her example, I wanted to develop a personal relationship with God. When I started to seek Him, beginning with my reading *The One Year Bible*, I began to understand my purpose in life. AnneMarie was one of the people I know God put in my path to help further my walk with Him. My relationship with AnneMarie helped me seek God and all His glory and to truly want to make a difference.

Upon reflection, it seems impossible to tell where AnneMarie's purpose and her generosity began and ended— they were so intertwined. Everything she did reflected her purpose, bringing individuals to relationship with each other and with God. Her generosity made her purpose-driven actions possible.

AnneMarie works in the medical field, but she finds time to serve as a chaplain at the hospital where she works. In a way, AnneMarie is like Mother Teresa, whose purpose was offering those in need the healing power of God's care, concern, and connection. Mother Teresa's willingness to share this gift with anyone who came her way was legendary. In fact, Mother Teresa gladly shared her hugs and caresses with those deemed contagious and consumed with dangerous diseases. Yet the nun's generosity shielded her with protection from such hurt, harm, and danger. She provided care and healing to society's most needy to the end of her days.

I witnessed that same throw-caution-to-the-wind attitude with AnneMarie's Christian walk. Our God is bigger than any problem, attitude, or person trying to find his or her way. I am so thankful that my father had a chance to meet AnneMarie on one of his visits with my mom to my home. AnneMarie invited us all to a church concert in which her good friend was performing. She insisted that we all ride in her little red Jeep! We thoroughly enjoyed the evening. AnneMarie has been and continues to be a generous blessing to me and countless others.

The Power of Generosity

We have each been uniquely blessed, and God wants us to be generous with our gifts, talents, and insights. Whatever your gifts are, God calls you to use them for the betterment of the world. Generosity is directly tied to living your purpose.

Practicing generosity as a way of life provides a daily dose of purpose renewal. Generosity originates from the same place as purpose: your heart. The act of giving and going beyond what is expected is an exercise of His will.

When I think back on times when I showed generosity to others, even though I may have been extremely busy, I ended up feeling better. That's because being in service to others is as foundational to our spiritual health as prayer. Nothing offers us an opportunity to serve others more than actions associated with generosity.

It warms the heart, reassures the soul, and boosts hope.

Have you ever been out to lunch and had your friend, quite unexpectedly, pay the whole tab? Have you had a complete stranger hold the door open for you or pick up something you dropped? Have you come home to flowers, a clean house, or a home-cooked meal?

We have all been witnesses to and direct recipients of sincere acts of generosity. Some are small yet profound. Others are among the most powerful experiences we have in our lives. Kindness begets kindness. Whether the action is spontaneous and random or planned and directed, it can ignite a chain reaction of good that expands exponentially.

GENEROSITY

Alana Stewart has worked in Hollywood for almost thirty years. I was particularly moved by my conversation with her and her commitment to helping her longtime friend Farrah Fawcett through her harrowing battle with cancer before her death in June 2009. Her generosity will inspire others to use some of their time being of service and giving back.

Alana Stewart
Actress, former model, and talk-show host.

Giving back, giving to others, and being of service best describe the concept of generosity to me. I find that people who are cheap with their money are cheap with their feelings and their emotions. Generosity is a way of thinking. Generosity is having an open heart. I certainly was not raised to think that way, and I think it is only in the last few years that I started to see the importance of giving back or generosity in my own life. My life seemed very small in that I was always focused on just my life, just my children and my family. I don't think it was until just really the last couple of years I sort of realized how important it is to really broaden that out, not just give to your children and the people around you that you love but to try to give back to life.

I think being generous helps me focus more on my goals. When you are more focused on your goals, you're a better manager of your time. I am a very ADD type of person. I get distracted very easily. I can have ten different directions I'm going in. I can be kind of scattered. I need one direction, and once I have that direction or that goal I can just be totally committed. I study different spiritual practices. I read lots of books on the subject. The root of many spiritual teachings is giving back. It's about being generous. I think it is very important to be of service. I've also been to twelve-step meetings. I won't say which one, but one of the cornerstones of twelve steps is service. When you focus on serving others, it puts things in perspective. It helps you be a better manager of your time. You schedule things so that you have time to give back and to be generous.

Being conscious of our time is so very important. I think it is one of the things I learned when I lost my friend Farrah Fawcett and others as well. Farrah's loss touched me, so closely. I lost my mother when I was much younger, but it was sudden, and it wasn't the same type of situation. Farrah's loss was watching someone I was very close to die of a disease that we were helpless to do anything about. That experience taught me to be very, very grateful for every second I am alive, and to cherish every second I have the people I love in my life.

Farrah was my best friend. I wrote a book about our experience looking for a cure for her cancer and making it my purpose to be with her a day at a time to do what I could do. That experience with her became a tremendous gift to me, and I really learned the value of being there for another person. In many ways, it taught me generosity, and only when I let go of being focused on my life did my life change. It really changed radically.

I'm working with the cancer foundation. Farrah was interested in helping people with cancer. Now, this work is more important to me than doing a TV show or other work in the entertainment business. I feel as though I have a bigger purpose. It all came about through my experience with Farrah.

The experience with Farrah Fawcett was a very difficult situation that not only helped me move forward, but also changed my life. It changed the way I look at everything in life. Giving or being generous with my time. Helping my friend really ended up helping me. I try to live in the moment now, not sweating the small stuff. I try to reach out and help others who are not in my immediate circle. It is a very rewarding feeling when you give to others. My experience in that situation helped me to see that.

It took me many years to get to this place in my life. There are things I wish I had taught my children when they were really young. There were things I did not know myself, like being in the moment. Enjoy today because you don't know. Life can change in a heartbeat. Love people. Really love them and appreciate them now. Someone who helped me a lot used to say, "Do one thing at a time. Stay in the moment. Don't look at the whole picture. Don't look at everything on your plate. Just walk through doing one thing at a time. Do what's before you and try to stay present." I think that is so important for all of us.

Another important thing is to conserve your energy. I know people who are running all the time. Maybe it's age and you can do it when you are younger, but for me I have to be focused. If I have a long busy day, I just want to eat, meditate, read something in one of my little spiritual books, look at something dumb on TV, then I'm re-energized.

Determination and faith are the tools that have been most beneficial to me. They are so different yet so connected. I think when things go wrong and times are bad, and it looks so dismal and you think it won't get better, that's when you have to have faith. That is when you have to have determination to keep going. You put one foot in front of the other and keep going.

For me, I believe very much in a higher power, in God. I believe that God has a way of working it out for us. Sometimes we just have to let go. I was raised with faith. It is not always easy for me, because I can get into fear. When I was young, I lived with my grandmother back in Texas, and we went to church. I have always believed in God. I think a belief in something bigger than yourself is really important. I believe there is a power and a presence I can turn to. My faith and my determination benefit me greatly.

Continue to Pay It Forward

As many people around the world have, you may have seen the movie *Pay It Forward*, where individuals gave in lavish and unsolicited ways to total strangers, demanding only one thing in return: that they do the same for someone else. The movie chronicled the power of a cheerful giver, and how the process transformed both the recipient and the giver.

Part of the story that isn't told, though, is how it's essential for the giver to be willing to make use of the moment at hand—to maximize each second. Often we have to decide, practically on the spot, whether we're going to look out for someone else or look the other way. You're standing on the street waiting for a cab. It's raining heavily and all the cabs that pass are fully occupied. Then you see a cabbie with a light on—finally! It pulls over, you reach to open the door, and out of the corner of your eye, you see an elderly couple trying to hail a cab. What do you do?

A small example, but that's the point. Every day we have opportunities to be generous. A man forgets his wallet in the car and is holding up the line at the grocery store. A legal secretary drops her entire carton of files on the subway. At home, the dishes are piled up to the size of a mountain in the sink. A mother with a stroller is trying to make it to her car while balancing children and groceries. We can sit and watch, justify that helping isn't our responsibility, or we can do something. Proverbs 3:27 reads, "Do not withhold good from those to whom it is due, when it is in your power to do it." We are commanded to "help the weak," and remember the words of the Lord Jesus, how He himself said, "It is more blessed to give than to receive" (Acts 20:35).

He wasn't telling us to give only to those we know, or to give only when we can afford it. He is calling us to be generous continually, making the most of every opportunity to show love and kindness to the people who cross our paths, whether we see them every day or only for a passing moment. We are called to give generously.

Pastor Rudy Rasmus of St. John's Downtown in Houston generously opened the doors of his church to me to facilitate a book club for the homeless, as I related in Chapter 1. The first book we read and discussed was *The Shack* by William P. Young (Windblown, 2007). *The Shack* is a compelling novel about a man struggling with grief after the tragic loss of his daughter and his finding courage to move past his judgments about why God allows his children to endure such pain and suffering. The way the experience touched participants was amazing. During our sessions, one lady insisted on reading an entire chapter aloud. Well, it happened to be one of the longest chapters in the book. Though everyone enjoyed the woman's enthusiasm, we had to stop her to get on with the discussion.

Discussing *The Shack* with the book club members was empowering in ways I never could have imagined. Though I had already been divested of the erroneous notion that all homeless persons were ignorant and lazy, I was still amazed at the insights participants shared. Some were exactly in line with my own thoughts. Others were so different they provided me with new ways of looking at things. Moreover, the confidence participants seemed to gain as their opinions were solicited and honored was priceless. I was reminded of how important it is for people to feel a sense of value and self-worth. I had not imagined that a book club would add to that experience. I just thought that since I enjoyed reading so much, there had to be homeless people who enjoyed reading as well. However, because of their living situation, I figured books were not readily available to them. I was exactly right about the passion for reading being alive and well in the hearts of the homeless persons I encounter, and I was pleasantly surprised at how the experience picked them up with a reminder of their worth and value. It was as if I could see their backs straighten and their sense of self-worth return.

Still, when people hear about me doing the book club, they mistakenly think that I was the only one playing the role of giver. Many of my friends said things like "Girl, that is so nice of you. You are so generous with your time to spend it with them." What they missed, however, was the fact that I was the biggest beneficiary of them all. Anything I was able to give to or share with the book-club members pales in comparison to the insights and fellowship they shared with me. In my mind, I was just the book girl—like Joy Behar from *The View* might say, "So what, who cares." But I would not trade seats with anyone. My audience was up close and personal and generously gave to me more than I ever could have given to them.

Acts of Goodness

In the late 1940s, Edith Irby Jones graduated from Knoxville College with bachelor's degrees in chemistry, physics, and biology. She became the first African American admitted to the University of Arkansas' medical school in Little Rock, and later its first graduate. However, before Irby graduated, she needed help and support from Little Rock's black community.

Daisy Bates, who would one decade later become the legendary champion of the Little Rock Nine, was a business owner and person of influence in the city. She generously became Irby's personal advocate and made sure all local businesses, churches, and families provided Irby Jones with the financial and social support she needed to complete her degrees.

Daisy and the other members of the Little Rock black community could easily have disregarded Irby, believing they had enough problems of their own. They could have used any number of excuses not to give. But their generosity paved the way for Irby not only to graduate, but also to become a legendary doctor who has traveled the world opening medical clinics for the underprivileged and training doctors all across Central and Latin America.

The best part about Irby's story to me is that her generous life of service was made possible by the generosity of others. Because she was given to, she, too, could give.

A Penny versus a Purse Full

Have you ever been to church on a Sunday when the pastor begins to preach about giving? It's one of my favorite sermons—and not necessarily because the pastor is particularly animated, but rather because of the congregation. I like to watch them. Once he begins speaking, all of a sudden it's as though red ants have invaded the pews. People get squirmy. They become uncomfortable. They look as though, if given the chance, they'd certainly run for the door.

Most of us don't like talking about money—at least not

the giving of it. Some of us have plenty, and we enjoy our plenty. Others of us have little and don't know how we could cope if the little became less. So we think it's better, easier, to keep our pocketbooks closed and to preach on things like hope and glory and other warm, fuzzy feelings.

While the gospel is certainly full of good news, it also contains the clear call to give, not simply of our time or skills, but also of our earthly wealth. This is for good reason. God didn't give us any directives that weren't intentional. When He told us to give what we were able, He had something very important in mind.

Consider the story of the widow in Mark. Jesus was watching people contribute to the offering box. Rich men sauntered down the aisles and gave large sums, but then a poor widow came and put in two small, copper coins, which made only a penny (Mark 12:42). Yet Jesus called His Disciples and said, "I tell you the truth, this poor widow has put more into the treasury than all the others. They gave out of their wealth; but she, out of her poverty, put in everything—all she had to live on" (Mark 12:43–44).

To me this story demonstrates the twofold power in generosity: by giving we provide for others, certainly, but perhaps even more so, by giving, we provide for ourselves. When we decide in our hearts to give, we free ourselves from the belief that money and material things are keys to our happiness. We open ourselves to genuine conversation about our purpose, about what gives us joy. By choosing generosity over selfishness, we choose people over possessions. We choose God's will over our own will. We are able to stop wasting our time and begin investing in relationships and God-ordained pursuits. Our 86400 becomes much more vibrant. Through generosity, we set off a chain reaction of good works, the total of which we may never be able to measure.

Think about the widow versus the rich men. By laying down her treasure, the widow told God, "I'm all in." The rich men, on the other hand, held their cards close to their chests and kept their savings in the bank. They didn't fully understand what they could receive if they truly gave.

Generosity is an indicator of our personal openness. We are telling God what He can and cannot put His hands on. By laying wide our time, talents, and money, we're telling God that we're all His, that we believe in His providence for our lives. But when we snap shut like the rich men in the story, we are telling God "Hands off!" When we keep worldly wealth close to our chests, we hold the wrong priorities. We believe more in what we have than in what God has promised us. When we pursue giving, a weight will be lifted off our chests. We will be able to focus our time and energy on the important things, and we will certainly feel the benefit in our health and in the happiness of simply loving others.

86400 Adviser: Jamie Foster Brown— Generosity

While Jamie Foster Brown, an entertainment magazine publisher, was still a child, her parents took in six children who had been abandoned temporarily by their mother. "We would see these kids all the time, with their faces pressed against their window looking outward," Brown said. "Inside, they had no furniture, no curtains, and no parents. After their stove caught fire and some of the kids were injured, my parents took them in and took care of them until they found their mother."

Although her parents did not have a lot of money, they shared what they had. "They have always shown concern for other people's children, for other people period," she said. "My concept of generosity comes from my parents. Generosity was modeled for me by my parents—my parents gave generously of themselves to those in need.

"Generosity is being kind," she continued. "It is being unselfish, giving of your time, your counsel, and your money to those who need it and those who seek it from you. I get the biggest joy out of making other people happy."

Others in her family set powerful examples, too. "My family, my grandmother, everyone in my family was always doing things for others, always being kind and generous," she said. "They were always teaching us how to be generous."

Brown showed early signs of adopting their spirit of generosity and values. She tells this story about experiencing the opportunity to be generous: "One day I was riding on my bicycle and I saw this big, fat juicy wallet just lying on the street. I was still a child at the time, and there was no one else around. I picked up the wallet and I took it to my parents. The wallet belonged to a lady not too far from where we lived. There was sixty-five dollars in it. That might not seem like a lot now, but that was a lot at the time. Back in the fifties, that was her rent, grocery money, everything. My dad took it down to her and told her that I'd brought it back. She was so grateful and wanted to give me five dollars as a reward, but my dad told her no. He told the lady that this was a blessing to his daughter because she got to learn an important lesson." It was the lesson of generosity.

Brown, the publisher and owner of *Sister 2 Sister*, a monthly entertainment magazine, dreams of one day turning her farm into a place for youngsters, an idea that grows out of her parents' example. She said the actions of her parents "set a standard in our house, which transferred to all areas of my life.

"My father would sit us down on Sundays on the sofa and give us all these rules and regulations on what's valuable and what's not, right and wrong," she recalled. "He taught us about consequences and the importance of a good work ethic. My mother was so sweet and so kind, we would say we could make pound cake out of her."

As an adult she also has been fortunate to find the same giving spirit in her husband of forty-one years, Lorenzo. He has a master's degree in math and a doctorate in economics and helps run her magazine. Their sons, Randy and Russell, work in the business as well. "My husband has been the person most beneficial to my success," she said. "He is the one who quit his job and supported me and works at my magazine. If I did not have this husband, I would not have this magazine. We daily feed off each other's ideas and interests. He is a sweet person, as sweet as he can be. He is an angel." Again, she is following her parents' example in living her marriage as a partnership based on generosity toward each other.

"I saw how my parents worked together and supported each other," she said. "They bought a store for nine hundred dollars and ran it together. They were a team. My husband and I are a team. Choosing the right mate is extremely important. I chose the right husband. He is so smart, and now he is working for me."

In her professional and personal lives, Brown is constantly

giving of her time, resources, and wisdom. While some people might regard that as a drain on their time and a waste of their 86400, to her it just makes good sense. "Taking time to be generous not only is the right thing to do, but it pays off, even if you are not looking for a payoff," she said. "Finding ways to be generous with your time is a good use of your time."

I first met Jamie Foster Brown at an NBA All-Star celebrity game, and I observed her as a stream of people, from well-known celebrities to readers of her magazine, constantly approached her. No matter who they were, she greeted them with a generous smile. As I have admired her over the years, I have seen the same generosity repeatedly.

As a media executive whose days are often extended by social obligations and travel, her time is so precious that she often works in the middle of the night. However, she feels she can still afford to share her 86400 when needed. "Sometimes I am called away from doing something important, but I choose to stop and do something that will help another," she said. "By doing this, helping someone, I can still be productive because feeling good about yourself and not having to worry about a friend's problem helps me to better concentrate on a task that requires my attention. In essence, I'm managing my time well, because I'm saving time by not worrying and being free to take care of my business."

Brown is also generous to herself, making time to stay fit, eat right, get rest, and look good, another lesson she learned from her father. "He always taught us that women had to smell good and dress well," she said.

Before founding *Sister 2 Sister* in 1988, Brown worked for Black Entertainment Television as an advertising secretary to its founder, Robert Johnson. She was subsequently promoted to producer for BET's flagship shows, *Video Soul* and *Video LP.*

Originally from Chicago, Brown is a graduate of the University of Stockholm (Sweden) and was awarded a doctorate in humane letters in 2008 from Bennett College. She attributes some of her success in business to willingness to devote the time needed and more to do a good job.

"You should be generous when working," she said. "If that employer hired you and promised to give you ten cents an hour, that is a contract, and you have to honor that. Always do more. Come early and leave late."

Since launching *Sister 2 Sister,* Brown said she is often the first to get interviews with major celebrities because her magazine treats them with respect. The articles are never mean-spirited and confrontational, even when they deal with controversial individuals or topics. Brown's publication also gives voice and exposure to many talented celebrities who have long been overlooked by Hollywood.

The publisher extends her generosity even to those who have not been so generous with her. Her fairy-tale rise from secretary at BET to producer of the network's two top-rated shows at the time sometimes triggered ugly jealousies, she said, but she chose not to retaliate. "One of the main people who was very hurtful towards me, I had the opportunity to recommend for a higher position," she said. "She did not like me at all, but I recommended her anyway." She did it with a smile, as she seems to do everything else. "My father told me that a smile goes a long way," she said. "He taught us that when you smile, you disarm (others). You make them feel good. If you are struggling in your career or trying to get a job, smile, be pleasant. Something that simple makes a big difference. You don't have to be the sharpest knife in the drawer, but being pleasant will take you a long way in good times and bad."

Extending kindness and generosity to others is the fulfillment of her purpose and is itself rewarding, she said. "It helps make me feel like I'm using my time for something positive and constructive, something that isn't self-seeking, but that sincerely works to better someone else's situation," she said. "My days are typically pretty busy, but when friends, family, or people come to me and need something, I think it's a number-one priority to help them. What better way can you spend your time than loving other people well?"

Your Next 600 Seconds

Devote your next 600 seconds to considering what it means to be generous and thinking of how you might be more generous. How can generosity help you fulfill your purpose and make the most of your 86400? What have people passed on to you that has proved valuable to your life? We sometimes forget that we are the recipients of countless acts of goodness and have the potential to be extravagant givers. Think of the most generous act you have ever done and how it made *you* feel. I challenge you to consider what you have received. It doesn't have to be money or material items. It often isn't, but we have all been blessed. How much more could you give? You might not be rich and you might not be a person of influence, but you can give of your time and of your talent. How can you become an extravagant giver who leaves a positive mark on someone else's life?

Seconds for the Spirit

"All the believers were together and had everything in common. Selling their possessions and goods, they gave to anyone as he had need. Every day they continued to meet together in the temple courts. They broke bread in their homes and ate together with glad and sincere hearts, praising God and enjoying the favor of all the people. And the LORD *added to their number daily those who were being saved"* (*Acts 2:44–47*).

10

Courage:
Bravery In Spite Of

*I learned that courage was not the absence
of fear, but the triumph over it. The brave
man is not he who does not feel afraid,
but he who conquers that fear.*
—Nelson Mandela

Courage is the fuel of the heart. It is the match that lights
the fire that illuminates the night. Without courage, we
would lack the wherewithal to pursue God's purpose.

Courage, for many, is a trip-up word. It's something we
think is only found in soldiers, firefighters, and police offi-
cers, those who walk directly into the face of all that is terri-
fying without flinching or retreating. We can't fathom how
courage could be a quality of a housewife, a college student,
or a business executive. We make the mistake of believing
that our lives are unfussy and that our pursuits are typical.
So while our life journeys might demand stamina and dedication, they certainly require courage as well.

Our lives demand just as much courage as the bravest of

the brave. Without courage, migrant workers would have been robbed of the leadership of Cesar Chavez. Without courage, women's suffrage might still be a pipe dream. Truly, nothing of consequence is done without courage.

Webster's New World College Dictionary defines *courage* as "the attitude of facing and dealing with anything recognized as dangerous, difficult, or painful, instead of withdrawing from it; quality of being fearless or brave; valor." Thus, courage is an attitude that you have to take on in order to press forward to do the difficult things in life. To me, courage is doing something you are afraid to do, don't really want to do, but that you know you must do. Courage is a state or mindset that you have to get into to do what you have to do.

It takes courage to fall in love, to give your heart with utmost sincerity to another. It takes courage to choose the desires of your soul over the pleadings of practicality, pursuing your dreams to be a writer, or a coach or chef, over being what everyone tells you that you ought to be. It takes courage to raise a family, to instill spiritual and moral guidance into the growing mind of a youngster, to choose continually the path of righteousness, to follow what is moral and upright, rather than what is often easy and socially acceptable. Apathy, complacency, anger, and selfishness are the birthmarks of the uncourageous. They are the easy outs in a difficult life, but to be humble, generous, kind, and forgiving takes courage. That is the mark of one of God's warriors.

Deep-Rooted Beliefs

When I was a child, I remember spending school recess out on the playground. That is the place where I could form friendships and latch on to another human being who could skip, swing, and trade sack lunches with me. While I was lucky enough to find a ragtag bunch with whom I could laugh and play games, I remember seeing other kids who were not so lucky. From the perspective of my classmates, the unlucky ones simply did not fit. They were pointed at and jeered as they searched for corners to hide in. They were the unwanted.

I knew, even then, that the way they were treated was unfair. I knew it was deeply wrong to treat another human being in such a lowly fashion. Being young and terrified of being jeered myself, I turned my head and continued to play my games, pretending as if the world around me didn't include children who ate alone and went home at night crying. It was amazing how easily I could block out their pain.

While those were the experiences of childhood, they translate very easily into our adult lives. How often have you found yourself in a position where you watched a friend do something you knew to be inappropriate or even immoral? How often have you watched a superior at work treat one of your co-workers unfairly? How often have you sat on the sidelines watching ridicule and faithlessness, scared to act because you might become the victim yourself? More importantly, how often have you participated in less-than-admirable activities? How often have you been the one to point the finger, to pass the blame, to turn your head and continue living your life while sin and pain abound in the periphery?

We have all been guilty of failing to live up to standards God calls us to uphold. We choose to acquiesce, rather than be firm in our beliefs. More often than not, this is because we lack courage. We worry too much about the repercussions of taking the higher ground and ultimately cower into routines of complacency and comfort that move us farther and farther away from living lives of intention. It is easy and uncourageous to be spiteful, angry, judgmental, greedy, and bitter. Conversely, it can often take our entire arsenal of strength to be compassionate, holy, sincere, and giving. The easy route, like the wide road, is paved with good intentions but few purpose-filled results.

Adventures in Africa

When I reflect on the principle of courage, what comes to mind immediately is one of my first trips to Angola, Africa, for two reasons. First, I took that trip with my best friend, 2010 Basketball Hall of Famer, WNBA legend, and Olympic Gold Medalist Cynthia Cooper, whose entire life has been a profile in courage. Second, meeting and mastering the challenges we faced during that international excursion demanded every ounce of courage we could muster.

As Cynthia's friend, I had often wondered if I had even an inkling of the courage she displayed so readily. I found my answer many years ago when she and I traveled to Angola.

Cynthia and I were very excited about our first trip together to Angola. My mother said that we were both very gutsy girls going to a country that was in the middle of a war and not knowing a single person from or living in Angola. We were determined to go and take medical supplies and goodwill, as well as look into prospective business ventures. We enlisted the help of two women who assured us that they would be our guides and assist us throughout the trip, thanks to their extensive list of Angolan contacts. Well, about two days into the trip, Cynthia and I figured out that the ladies did not have the connections or the expertise regarding Angola they suggested. Far more disturbing was the fact that these women, who shall remain nameless, took half of the medical supplies, toys, and other items to stuff their own pockets.

They had told us it was customary to supply some form of aid to their country if you sought to do business. Cynthia and I had no problem with that, since both of us had long histories of community service and eagerly wanted to help in any way possible. Far from viewing the request as an imposition, we viewed it as a blessing, as another way to give back. Cynthia and I secured at least $75,000 worth of goods that really became the focus of our trip even more than setting up any new business ventures. We soon became aware, however, that our supplies were not being delivered to hospitals in Angola. Upon investigation, we found out that our guides used at least half of the goods we collected to sell for personal profit. We also found out that Cynthia and I were not the first persons fooled by their ruse. We were told that these women regularly persuaded Americans to secure goodwill supplies that they would then sell.

Amazingly, we were able to get the authorities to recover most of the goods and get them to their intended destination as gifts. The subsequent confrontation we had with the women in the middle of the hotel lobby was like a scene out of a movie and was not for the faint of heart. Cynthia was the one who had the courage to face off with them directly.

Though the women denied any wrongdoing, a gentleman we befriended showed the authorities where the goods were, but we had to fend for ourselves from then on because the women had controlled all the arrangements and logistics for our time in Angola, our pending visit to South Africa, and for our trip home. To get the supplies to the right destinations and to carry on took tremendous courage on both of our parts.

God was revealing to me that I had a reserve of courage, and I was becoming more and more comfortable displaying it. Being stuck in Angola is not like being left at the neighborhood mall. Yet I knew with every fiber of my being that Cynthia and I would be all right. My friend later shared with me that my calm demeanor in the face of the betrayal had encouraged her. Imagine that! There I was feeling empowered by my friend's I'll-take-on-a-bear-at-any-time attitude, and she was being strengthened by what she called my quiet strength.

We managed to stay "on purpose" and fulfill the most important objectives of our trip. We made contact with the Angolan Foundation (FESA) and other charitable outreach organizations. I forged lasting relationships that led to my becoming a founding board member of the Houston/Angola Sister City Organization. Later, I was elected as the first president of the organization. Eventually we made our way to South Africa, but not without more obstacles, and eventually home. Through it all, we had to rely on our courage. I was fortunate to have Cynthia with me as a role model and friend.

My Brave Friend

If it seems you've had more obstacles than opportunities in your life, or if your best efforts feel as though they will never be enough, Cynthia Cooper knows where you've been. Long before she led the WNBA's Houston Comets to four consecutive championships, claimed two WNBA MVP awards, and won several ESPY Awards, Cynthia faced a life of poverty and frustration, hungering for dreams that seemed way out of reach.

Though a stand-out player at USC, Cynthia's athletic promise took a backseat to pain when her brother died. Dropping out of school for a short time to cope with her loss, she returned only to find herself again in the shadows— this time of players who received much more press. Undeterred, Cynthia completed a successful collegiate career. Yet her dreams of playing professional basketball in the U.S. seemed foolish. Women with such ambitions were then limited to overseas teams. The majority of female collegiate athletes forgo their dreams of playing the sport they love in order to find a more practical occupation. Cynthia faced the same pressures, yet courageously chose to follow her heart by traveling to Europe to play in their women's professional basketball circuit, which she did successfully for eleven years.

Miraculously, the WNBA was founded, providing female basketball players a stateside professional career option. Yet Cynthia was long past the point in her career at which the average player has already retired. To realize her dream, she had to bet on her abilities to compete successfully against athletes who were much younger than she was. Cynthia's courage paid off as she not only competed, but dominated, during her WNBA career.

Yet success on the court did not protect Cynthia from painful realities off court as her mother suffered through breast cancer. During this period, Cynthia discovered the day-to-day courage she needed to help her mother battle the most formidable of opponents. Her mother lost her battle, and, shortly thereafter, Cynthia's very good friend and Houston Comet teammate Kim Perrot died of cancer as well. Still, Cynthia persevered and served as a mentor and role model for younger players while remaining at the top of her game.

Upon her retirement, she took on the challenge of a career path in which she had much less experience than her peers: coaching. Again Cynthia emerged courageous and victorious, turning around the Prairie View A&M University Women's Basketball program as head coach. Recently, Cynthia took the reins as head coach of the North Carolina–Wilmington's women's basketball team. I can't wait to see her in action. I'm more than confident that she will be a huge success.

COURAGE

Mike Feinberg is co-founder of the Knowledge Is Power Program (KIPP), a network of fifty-seven public charter schools across the United States serving poor and minority students. Years ago, I was an instructional supervisor in the Houston Independent School District. As part of that job, I was one of the trainers who trained and supervised Teach for America teachers. Mike Feinberg and his KIPP co-founder, Dave Levin, were in that first class of 200 or so teachers. As I have watched their progress, I've been very proud of what they do to make a difference in children's lives.

Mike Feinberg
Co-founder of Knowledge Is Power Program (KIPP).

I think courage is having a specific goal or aspiration or vision, and then doing whatever it takes to reach it, not letting fear, doubts, or disbeliefs get in the way. It's not about how to eliminate fears, doubts, or disbeliefs, because there will always be fears, doubts, and disbeliefs. Courage is taking that step despite all of the uncertainties that are inside each and every one of us. Courage helps you to be a better manager of time because it helps you to avoid the quicksand. Courage helps you avoid inaction and the inability to make decisions. The inability to make decisions leads to a whole bunch of issues and problems. At that point, people have to spend time working on issues and problems that they would not have had to spend time on if they simply had the courage to make better decisions in the first place.

Time, more than anything else, is the limiting factor. We can become smarter. We can become more efficient. We can become better. We can change our attitude—all those things are within our spheres of influence to work on, but what we do not have the ability to do, no matter how hard we try, is that we will never ever be able to add a twenty-fifth hour to the day. That makes time a limiting resource. If time is a limited resource, that makes time a precious resource. You had better maximize it, because we don't have unlimited amounts of it.

Grit and persistence are essential for me to keep going, never quitting, and always having the humility to admit when I've made a mistake. I just keep working at it and working at it.

By definition I'm an introvert. I am one point away from being as far out on that introvert scale as you can possibly get, but for me, what makes up for that is courage. Before I speak publicly, I have to say a little prayer to myself. I remind myself that this is all about the kids. That's how I'm able to get up on that stage. You know, I have to spend energy talking to people, but my natural state is not talking. My wife and son are the opposite. My son won't stop talking. He gets that from his mother.

Advice I give to people who are struggling is that I find it's always better to regret what you have done instead of what you haven't done. Of course the caveat there is people should still have strong values and character. The second thing is searching out and understanding what floats your boat. There are things to do and causes to believe in that get each and every one of us out of bed and excited. My suggestion would be to find those causes, find the work, find what floats your boat, and find a way to turn that into what you do with your life.

Spiritual Superheroes

Courage can be so helpful as you seek to maximize your 86400. Acts of courage order your steps in a very directed and focused way. Whether in the world of fantasy or reality, acts of courage move people to action right now! In the lexicon of superheroes, the two who have proven most popular and enduring with children, teens, and adults are Batman and Spiderman. Even more so than the Man of Steel, Batman and Spiderman have found a place in the hearts of many because they both exhibit courage that speaks to us in the real world.

Although Batman's alter ego, the rich and dashing playboy billionaire Bruce Wayne, has little in common with us, he is motivated daily by the painful loss of his parents when he was a youth. In addition, unlike most superheroes, Batman has absolutely no special powers. Even though he faces the same villains that back even Superman into a corner, Batman courageously battles his own pain and his own shortcomings as he defends the defenseless.

In Spiderman's case, he became a hero when he was a high-school science whiz who was unpopular with the ladies and untalented athletically. He too suffered a painful loss of a loved one that inspires him. More than any superhero before or since, he is part of story lines that are dominated as much by his battles over shyness and financial troubles as they are by his battles against his archenemies. In both cases, we, the readers, connect to people who are making the most of their 86400, and using courage to do so—courage not only to battle bad guys, but courage to battle their own issues, fears, and pains.

The battles of biblical heroes can also inspire us to muster up courage to face our own challenges and make the most of our 86400.

One example is the tale of the Maccabees and their great endurance, which was recorded in writings that are not recognized as part of the Bible by Protestants, but are included by Catholics and some other Christian churches as part of the Old Testament.

The Maccabean War, a twenty-five-year battle, was fought by a band of peasant farmers and priests against the Greeks, then the most powerful army in the world. Mattathias, the high priest of the country town of Modein, along with his five sons, led the Maccabees through the war and to an inevitable truce—a period of relative peace for the once lowly Hebrews.

In the First Book of the Maccabees, Mattathias lay on his deathbed as the war loomed on, no end in sight. He gathered his sons around him and told them to "take courage, and behave manfully in the law: for by it you shall be glorious" (1 Macc. 2:64, New Advent Bible, online version). He told his sons if they stood up for what they believed, they would receive more glory than they ever would making money, earning a title or position, or winning fame.

To the dying priest, courage was priceless because it moved men and women of conviction off the sidelines, off the straddled fence, and into the ball game—into action. Courage pushed individuals to maximize their time to do something—anything—besides sit still and watch events unfold. Courage led people to live their purpose.

Mattathias' conviction, though centuries old, is extremely valuable in the modern context. To this day, we all are rooted in beliefs. There are things we feel strongly about and that keep our motors charged and running. The question is, What will we do for those beliefs?

In our convictions, we all have a decision to make. Are we going to be passive spectators, watching idly from our comfortable seats as the action unfolds? Or are we going to become a vital part to the transformation of this world? Will we, like the Maccabees, choose to stand up against nearly insurmountable odds? Our daily decision to be engaged participants, to peel back change like layers of an onion, is a crucial part of using courage to make the most of our 86400. Without the courage to take action, our most passionate beliefs will merely turn to idle thoughts or the famous but highly useless good intentions.

86400 Adviser: Bill Cosby — Courage

Bill Cosby found courage when he was nineteen years old and joined the U.S. Navy as a high-school dropout who had run out of options. "I quit high school at age nineteen with no degree," said the now legendary entertainer. "That put me in a compromising position. I do not recommend this. I was standing in my neighborhood looking at two extremes: old people or little children. That's because all my friends had finished school and went into the service or college. There was nobody for me to play with, so I joined the navy. I joined the navy for what reason? Because I did not know how to do anything. By age nineteen, I had not taken responsibility."

In a way, that was his first courageous act. "When I joined the service it was because I had rejected the responsibility of the homework, of the studying, of being a student," he recalled. "I could not see clearly and did not want to see clearly."

Growing up in a housing project in Philadelphia, William Henry Cosby, Jr., the son of a maid and a navy serviceman, had gotten through school clowning and doing as little as possible, he said, and he could get away with it. His father was away in the military for much of his childhood, and his mother worked twelve hours a day. "When I got to sixth grade, I had a teacher who was very, very stern," he said. "She was on me so I had to perform. I had to do it, and [before her] I did as little as I had to do to keep that teacher off my back. She would say do a report on So-and-so, so I had to do it. 'So-and-so was born, and then he died. The end.'"

As that sixth-grade teacher stayed on him, he excelled. However, when the end of the year came, he said, "On my report card she wrote, 'I'm afraid that if William does not have someone on him, he will go back to his old habits.'" His teacher's worst fears were realized when he was promoted to the next grade. "When I hit seventh grade, nobody was there to stay on me," he said. "Understand me; I'm not talking about it was their fault. That teacher predicted that I was going to fail. She knew that I could be successful, but I really wasn't there yet, because I did not accept responsibility."

In tenth grade, he flunked out. When he found himself in the navy, he said, "I had to wake up at 4:30 a.m. I belonged to the government. So that was my wake-up call."

It seemed that he could hear the voices of every elder who had tried to tell him throughout his life that he had potential. "All the people who told me I was very, very bright," he said, "those voices came just in a giant smoke that covered my body.

"At that point, I woke up and began to devote myself to doing better; to taking responsibility," he said. "When I started to pull from those past lessons, I began to work hard. I experienced success because I decided to take responsibility."

He mustered the courage to finish his high-school requirements through correspondence courses, attended Temple University on an athletic scholarship, and completed a doctorate in education from the University of Massachusetts in 1976.

It took courage to take action and finally pursue a real education.

While he was at Temple, he had started doing the stand-up comedy routines that eventually led to his spectacular rise to stardom. Each step—from his pioneering role on *I Spy* as one of the few blacks seen on television in the 1960s to creating the cartoon series *Fat Albert* in the 1970s and producing such original series as *The Cosby Show* in the 1980s— demanded the courage to go where others had not.

More recently, it took tremendous courage for him to embark on and defend the book he wrote with Dr. Alvin F. Poussaint, *Come On, People: On the Path from Victims to Victors* (Thomas Nelson, 2007). While the book challenges African Americans to take responsibility to solve many of the problems they encounter as a race, some scholars, leaders, and ordinary black people attacked it as selling out, airing dirty laundry, or blaming the victim. Through it all, Cosby stood his ground, facing cameras, probing commentators, or hostile live audiences again and again. The main reason I wanted to interview him was that he has been an outspoken advocate for education, an interest that has been a major focus of my life and career.

"Having courage requires you to see things differently," Cosby said. "If you have the apathy, the depression, and all of the cousins that go along with it—the inertia, the entropy, all of these negative things—you can't believe that you can move forward to take a step. You are afraid because of whatever is in you. Courage, for people who are in that depression, in that apathy, needs stimulation. They need stimulation of the positive."

He said that courage wears many cloaks. "Sometimes when applied to a battered woman, you have to have the courage to leave that man who is beating you up," he said. "Having courage takes you a step away from that which is the wrong comfort zone in your life. Now, to discourage you, your mind can say, 'If I go away he will find me,' so you will stay. You are discouraged. However, if I can get you to community college, you still need to be encouraged, because your old feelings of discouragement still reside, your old habits."

For him, Cosby said, courage requires that woman "to throw away discouragement and to invite encouragement, to stay stimulated; to continue to walk forward, feeling good about what one is doing and knowing that one must continue. One must believe that this is the comfort zone on the way to success."

To make that move also requires education, Cosby argues. "Moving from thought to action requires education of self, formal education, education about your history, communication with elders, the wise, and the courage to take steps," said Cosby. "All of these things help you move from thought to action."

Sometimes it takes a "pep talk" or cheerleading to encourage people to move forward. Encouragement is "stimulation of the positive," Cosby said. "Stimulation, encouragement to bring the team to victory. So we need—people need—encouragement that helps to bring forth or stimulate you to believe and have the courage to take that step towards that goal, that dream.

"Being conscious of your 86400 is a way for you to check yourself," he said. "It is important for you to check and lift yourself up according to your field. You know churches do it every Sunday. They do it through Jesus. They keep telling you that Jesus is strong. Your seconds in a day require—through the Bible, through philosophy—that you encounter and stay with people and around people who can give you sound philosophy and encourage you to go up, to challenge yourself without being afraid."

In other words, to have courage. Cosby said prayer helps him to tap into his store of courage, carry out his purpose, and maximize his 86400. "I wake up and start each day with how I went to sleep last night—with a prayer," he said. "Start with a prayer. Finish with a prayer. My suggestion to people on starting each day, each 86400, is give yourself a prayer of encouragement—not one where you hope, but give yourself a realization prayer. Get on your knees or lie in the bed and look up into the darkness or hug your wife or something, and say to yourself, 'This is who I am. This is who I'm going to be—a better person. I'm going to do this. I have things that I have to do because I want to be better.'"

The experience of talking one on one with one of my all-time favorite entertainers who just happens to be one of the foremost education and purpose-management advocates in the world gave me a boost of courage and encouragement to keep dreaming big and believing all things are possible.

Your Next 600 Seconds

Devote your next 600 seconds to evaluating how courage can help you to move forward and make the most of your God-given time. Has fear held you back from doing something you wanted or needed to do? Has discouragement kept you from stepping out on faith? Envision yourself doing something that would have terrified you not too long ago. Are you at a standstill and would having more courage break you out of it? Courage doesn't always look like we expect it to. It doesn't come walking into the room with large, powerful muscles. In your own life, who would you consider courageous? If you have the courage to follow what you know to be true, consider how much more rewarding—both spiritually and emotionally—your life could be.

Seconds for the Spirit

> *"He shall say: 'Hear, O Israel, today you are going into battle against your enemies. Do not be faint-hearted or afraid; do not be terrified or give way to your panic before them. For the* LORD *your God is the one who goes with you to fight for you against your enemies to give you victory'"* (Deut. 20: 3–4).

Conclusion

Unlimited Purpose

Living an 86400-focused life has allowed me the opportunity to get the most out of a limited resource—"time"—and remove all limits, barriers, and hindrances to my dreams, aspirations, and goals. I live life each day open to the infinite possibilities that come when my actions carry the heft and power of purpose.

The transition from mere time management to incorporating the ten purpose characteristics in my life put me in a place mentally, emotionally, and spiritually where I could see success.

My first challenge to you is to incorporate the purpose characteristics of: Forgiveness, Wisdom, Dedication, Balance, Imagination, Thankfulness, Patience, Faithfulness, Generosity, and Courage into your daily 86400. Incorporating the characteristics I've discussed will challenge you to look at your life not from a distant, objective, scholarly perspective, but from a down-and-dirty, real-deal, front-row seat. The purpose values will minister to you daily, keeping you in line and on track. However, these values are merely hollow concepts if they are not placed in conversation with the things that affect your life in deep and profound ways—the past we carry, the present we live, the future we seek, and the life we're intended to lead.

Each of us is impacted by events and experiences of our past, the demands of our present, the hopes and dreams of our future, and the gnawing notions of the life we're intended to lead. To attempt to maximize productiveness and purpose without recognizing these realities would be akin to attempting to swim without water. No matter how much energy you expend, you are still not really getting anything done. We all need the honest remembrances and introspection brought on by dealing with issues, challenges, and opportunities afforded us by our past, present, and future dreams to truly fuel the fire to make the most of the ten purpose characteristics.

Forgiveness is a powerful tool that enables us to let go of things from the past that impede progress and keep us from moving forward toward our purpose.

Wisdom is learning from the past so that you know what to do in the present, and then doing it to create a better future.

Dedication calls for us to take the long view of life and order our present steps so they move us toward the life we are intended to lead. Often such dedication is kick-started by reflections on the ways that were made for you by others in the past.

Balance puts you in a state of harmony and inner peace that can allow you to weather life's storms as well as enjoy its victories.

Imagination is God's gift to us to explore what He has created. Imagination allows us to plug into divine purpose.

Thankfulness is, at its core, what happens when we understand the value of what we have. Being thankful wards off negativity the way insect repellent wards off bugs. Thankfulness reminds us of the power of our blessings and the magnificence of God's love.

Patience allows you to take a deep breath, create a game plan with a clear head, and sincerely enjoy the process of achieving your desires. Patience gives us all the time we need to become the people God intends us to be.

Faithfulness inspires us to persevere and continue working toward our not-yet-achieved reality in spite of doubts and fatigue. Faithfulness is displaying so much confidence in the "not yet" reality, the "not yet" achieved goal, or the "not yet" life desired that you act as if it already is.

Generosity originates from the same place as purpose—your heart. Practicing generosity as a way of life provides a daily dose of purpose renewal. The act of giving and going beyond what is expected is an exercise of His will.

Courage pushes individuals to maximize their time to do something—anything—but sit still and watch events unfold.

Writing this book has been a ministry and a therapeutic and liberating process—a blessing that did not stop once my fingers ceased typing. You will not be alone as you begin living an 86400-focused life, making the most of every second of each day. I, along with the 86400 advisers and supporters, will be with you, supporting you as you journey into 86400 days filled with promise, unlimited possibilities, and, most importantly, purpose.

The 86400 concept has sparked the 86400 Seconds Movement, which continues to motivate me and will aid you as you move from thought to action.

The 86400 Movement Web site (www.86400movement
.com) contains personal testimonies, additional 86400 advisers, and more examples of how individuals from all walks of
life are connecting with the 86400 concept to live their lives
on purpose. 86400 Seconds seminars, journals, companion
books, and workbooks will soon be available to assist, motivate, and inspire you to live the life you are intended to live.

The incredible feedback from the 86400 Seconds Movement opened a door of opportunity to me to develop
the *86400 Book Club for Kids* that appears monthly on
KRIV-TV, Fox 26 in Houston. As an educator by trade, I
am always looking for new ways to touch and inspire children to get excited about the learning process. The good
people at KRIV-TV viewed the 86400 concept as a way to
speak to kids and their parents, as an instigator to get them
excited about making the most of their days by spending
some of those precious seconds reading good books.

You can follow the 86400 Movement on Facebook and
Twitter and discover the 86400 apps whereby the most
technologically challenged or savvy can get in where they
fit in and join the movement to make every second of every
day count.

The business, corporate, civic, and community partners
of this growing 86400 Movement are a testimony to the
divine power such an approach offers. Individuals I have
admired and respected for their work as actors, elected offi-
cials, community servants, and business professionals have
joined the 86400 team. The growth and expansion of the
86400 Movement has been nothing short of amazing, and
new ideas for expansion come each and every day. I will
share with you one of my future goals for expanding the
influence and outreach of this movement, which also incor-

porates my second challenge to you: I want you to join the movement, get involved. I can't wait to meet you and work with you!

As an educator, I am disturbed by what is going on with our educational system. The number of dropouts in our country is a statistical entity to some, but a hard reality to others. I have seen the personal, mental, and emotional destruction wrought by educational failure. When I followed a time-management approach to my days, I would have been convinced that I had little or no room on my schedule to do anything about it. However, purpose management, living an 86400-focused life, reminds me that meeting this challenge is in keeping with my purpose. I envision recruiting good citizens to get involved in the education of children in their community by becoming 86400 coaches or advisers in K–12 schools. The 86400 Movement will provide necessary screening and training. These coaches will be ordinary citizens trained as mentors, big brothers and sisters, and helpers to assist. One of the most glaring gaps in schools and thus educational success for students is parental involvement. Where parental involvement is high, student achievement is high. However, not every child has parents or guardians able to give what is necessary to make a meaningful difference in their child's education. Teachers are being called on to be teachers, parents, social workers, counselors, and even legal advocates for children.

The 86400 coach would provide encouragement, motivation, tutoring, and serve as a role model and mentor to students, helping them take the responsibility for their own education. My vision is for every K–12 student who needs one to have an 86400 coach. These individuals would not take the place of counselors, but, as screened professionals, would stick with the student through his or her educational career.

People dedicated to making every second of every day count can make this vision a reality. Join the 86400 Movement. I want your commitment. Together let's move forward confidently, from thought to action, living our lives on purpose, and making the most of each and every blessed gift of our 86400 seconds.

Sources

Chapter 1: Forgiveness
"To forgive is to set a prisoner free and discover that the prisoner was you." Lewis B. Smedes, Christian author and theologian (from www.brainyquote.com).

Chapter 2: Wisdom
"A good traveler has no fixed plans and is not intent on arriving." Laozi, ancient Chinese philosopher considered the father of Taoism (from www.brainyquote.com).

Chapter 3: Dedication
"The need for devotion to something outside ourselves is even more profound than the need for companionship. If we are not to go to pieces or wither away, we must have some purpose in life; for no man can live for himself alone." Ross Parmenter (from "The Doctor and the Cleaning Woman," *The Plant in My Window*).

Chapter 4: Balance
"Happiness is not a matter of intensity but of balance, order, rhythm and harmony." Thomas Merton, author and Trappist monk (from www.brainyquote.com).

Chapter 5: Imagination

"Fairy tales are more than true: not because they tell us that dragons exist, but because they tell us dragons can be beaten." G. K. Chesterton, as quoted in *Coraline* (2002), by Neil Gaiman.

Chapter 6: Thankfulness

"I thank God for my handicaps, for, through them, I have found myself, my work, and my God." Helen Keller, author and activist (from www.worldfamousquotes.net).

Chapter 7: Patience

"The two most powerful warriors are patience and time." Lev Nikolayevich Tolstoy, Russian moral thinker, novelist, and philosopher (from www.thinkexist.com).

Chapter 8: Faithfulness

"Listen to the mustn'ts, child. Listen to the don'ts. Listen to the shouldn'ts, the impossibles, the won'ts. Listen to the never haves, then listen close to me—Anything can happen, child. Anything can be." Shel Silverstein, *Where the Sidewalk Ends*, 1974.

Chapter 9: Generosity

"Do all the good you can,
By all the means you can,
In all the ways you can,
In all the places you can,
At all the times you can,

To all the people you can,
As long as ever you can."
—John Wesley, theologian and founder of the Methodist
movement, "Rule of Conduct," *Letters of John Wesley* (from
www.quotationsbook.com).

Chapter 10: Courage
"I learned that courage was not the absence of fear, but the
triumph over it. The brave man is not he who does not feel
afraid, but he who conquers that fear." Nelson Mandela, former president of South Africa (from www.woopidoo.com).

Visit the 86400 Seconds Movement @ www.86400
movement.com. Text 86400 to 90210 to get the latest
updates regarding Purpose Management and the 86400
Movement.

Reading List

H. Jackson Brown, Jr., *Life's Little Instruction Book* (Thomas Nelson, 2000).

Brennan Manning, *The Ragamuffin Gospel: Good News for the Bedraggled, Beat-Up, and Burnt Out* (Multnomah Books, 1993).

John Eldredge, *Wild at Heart: Discovering the Secret of a Man's Soul* (Thomas Nelson, 2001).

The One Year Bible (Tyndale House, 1986).

Malcolm Gladwell, *Outliers* (Little, Brown and Company, 2008).

Ralph de la Vega, *Obstacles Welcome: Turn Adversity into Advantage in Business and Life* (Thomas Nelson, 2009).

Sherri Shepherd, *Permission Slips: Every Woman's Guide to Giving Herself a Break* (Grand Central Publishing, 2009).

Jerry de Jaager and Jim Ericson, *See New Now: New Lenses for Leadership and Life* (Bergen Publishing, 2009).

Daymond John, *Display of Power: How FUBU Changed a World of Fashion, Branding and Lifestyle* (Thomas Nelson, 2007).

Andrew Newberg and Mark Robert Waldman, *How God Changes Your Brain: Breakthrough Findings from a Leading Neuroscientist* (Ballantine, 2010).

Bill Cosby and Dr. Alvin F. Poussaint, *Come On, People: On the Path from Victims to Victors* (Thomas Nelson, 2007).

Roland Martin, *Listening to the Spirit Within: 50 Perspectives on Faith* (Romar Media Group, 2007).

Paula White, *You're All That!: Understand God's Design for Your Life* (FaithWords, October 2007).

Alana Stewart, *My Journey with Farrah: A Story of Life, Love, and Friendship* (HarperCollins Publishers, 2009).

Clift and Kathleen Richards, *Bible Prayers for All Your Needs* (Victory House, 1999).

Pastor Rudy Rasmus, *Touch: Pressing Against the Wounds of a Broken World* (Thomas Nelson, 2008).

Marcos Witt, *How to Overcome Fear: And Live Your Life to the Fullest* (Atria, 2007).